PROJECT AIR FORCE

T0288697

Evaluating the Impact of a Total Force Service Commitment Policy on Air Force Pilot Manning

An Exploratory Application of Inventory Modeling

David Schulker, Tara L. Terry

Prepared for the United States Air Force

For more information on this publication, visit www.rand.org/t/RR2400

Library of Congress Cataloging-in-Publication Data is available for this publication.
ISBN: 978-1-9774-0029-1

Published by the RAND Corporation, Santa Monica, Calif.

© Copyright 2018 RAND Corporation

RAND® is a registered trademark.

Support RAND
Make a tax-deductible charitable contribution at
www.rand.org/giving/contribute

www.rand.org

Preface

The Air Force faces a severe shortage of pilots and career enlisted aviators that senior leaders have described as an "aircrew crisis." In March 2017, the Air Force Deputy Chief of Staff for Manpower, Personnel, and Services testified before Congress that the Total Force manned pilot shortage at the end of fiscal year 2016 was 1,555 pilots, most of whom resided in the fighter community (Grosso, 2017). The projected increase in major airline job opportunities and increasing pay for civilian pilots in the major airlines will likely hamper efforts to resolve this issue. Additionally, some pilots in communities in which the shortages are most severe are increasingly dissatisfied with their operational tempo and assignments. Given these shortages and expected retention challenges, the Air Force is investigating ways to increase retention among these critical and expensive-to-train operators.

Air Force leaders have recognized that aggressive policies will be needed to deal with the pilot shortage in the long term and are looking at a myriad of options and their potential outcomes. The Director of Training and Readiness (AF/A3T) therefore asked RAND Project AIR FORCE to examine one potential policy option: a Total Force (rather than component-specific) service commitment with increased service commitment lengths. This report documents RAND's efforts to develop a Total Force service commitment model and explains its unique features and inputs, as well as exploratory results and implications for the policy at hand.

This report provides information about the development of a statistical model for retention under longer service commitments, as well as modeling changes required to address a modified Palace Chase program and a Total Force service commitment. It should interest those concerned with technical modeling aspects of career field health planning and those concerned about retention of the pilot force.

This research was commissioned by the U.S. Air Force and conducted within the Manpower, Personnel, and Training Program of RAND Project AIR FORCE as part of a fiscal year 2016 project, Total Force Aircrew Management Analytic Support. The work was originally shared with the U.S. Air Force on April 27, 2017. The draft report, issued on September 25, 2017, was reviewed by formal peer reviewers and U.S. Air Force subject-matter experts.

RAND Project AIR FORCE

RAND Project AIR FORCE (PAF), a division of the RAND Corporation, is the U.S. Air Force's federally funded research and development center for studies and analyses. PAF provides the Air Force with independent analyses of policy alternatives affecting the development, employment, combat readiness, and support of current and future air, space, and cyber forces. Research is conducted in four programs: Force Modernization and Employment; Manpower, Personnel, and

Training; Resource Management; and Strategy and Doctrine. The research reported here was prepared under contract FA7014-16-D-1000.

Additional information about PAF is available on our website:
www.rand.org/paf/

Contents

Figures

Summary

Background and Purpose

There is a high level of concern among senior Air Force leaders about projected aircrew shortages, which are so severe they have been labeled an "aircrew crisis." The Air Force currently has too few pilots to fill required positions, and these projected shortages could worsen in the future if trends continue. These shortages coincide with a new boom in the labor market for civilian air transport pilots, where hiring opportunities have been shown to draw pilots out of the Air Force. The potential Air Force responses to these challenges are straightforward: produce (and absorb) more pilots, reduce the number of requirements, increase retention, or some combination of the three. However, the effects of any policy changes must also consider ripple effects in the reserve components (RCs; the Air National Guard and Air Force Reserve), because they rely mainly on prior service Regular Air Force (RegAF) pilots who separate and affiliate with one of the RCs.

In light of these challenges, the Air Force asked RAND Project AIR FORCE to evaluate whether a Total Force service commitment (TFSC) policy could reduce or eliminate the pilot shortage. Such a policy would replace the current active duty service commitment and reserve service commitment of 10 years with a TFSC longer than 10 years. The TFSC policy also modifies the Palace Chase program, which allows RegAF pilots under an active duty service commitment to transfer to the RC. Essentially, the new TFSC policy would attach a single, component-agnostic service commitment to newly winged pilots and permit the level of cross-flow that best addresses the Total Force shortages.

Approach

To evaluate whether a TFSC policy would offset the pilot shortage, we modified RAND's Total Force Blue Line (TFBL) model, which projects future pilot numbers by aging the population over time using programmed production, and projected losses and affiliations (Terry et al., forthcoming). TFBL output allows users to compare the projected number of each type of pilot that remains in each component in future years with the number of requirements by pilot type to assess manning health.[1] TFBL can also determine the optimum levels of production and affiliations to achieve several goals under certain assumptions of loss and affiliation rates. We altered this model to gauge the effects of the proposed TFSC policy; the modifications include

---

[1] We use the terms *manning* and *manning health* to refer to the degree to which there are enough pilots available to meet existing and projected job requirements.

adjustments to loss and affiliation behavior to assess scenarios involving increased service commitment lengths, as well as building an explicit and modified Palace Chase path to the RCs.[2] In essence, the TFSC policy holds pilots in their respective components longer while opening a window of time where pilots can transfer from the RegAF to the RCs if doing so meets policy goals. The policy goals that undergird the modeling include the four baseline goals of the TFBL (all receiving equal weight) and one other goal governing Palace Chase utilization (which was assigned an additional penalty to reflect career field management aims after deliberation with action officers). They are as follows:

- **Meet as many requirements as possible:** Minimize requirements that cannot be filled with a qualified pilot in a given component/community each fiscal year (FY).
- **Minimize overages:** Minimize excess pilots who cannot be matched to an open requirement in a given component/community each FY.
- **Minimize production:** Produce the fewest number of pilots possible while meeting other goals each FY.
- **Follow historical affiliation norms:** Match historical affiliation patterns as closely as possible when affiliating or transferring pilots from the RegAF to the RCs each FY.
- **Use Palace Chase as a last resort:** Minimize the use of Palace Chase transfers while meeting other goals each FY.

A revised TFSC policy could reduce pilot shortages across the Total Force in two ways. First, inventory levels could improve in all components, because longer service commitments increase the average amount of time pilots remain in service. Second, RC inventories could benefit from expanded Palace Chase utilization if surplus RegAF pilots who do not separate can be transferred to RC communities in need.

In estimating plausible loss and affiliation patterns under longer service commitments, we exploit the fact that pilots complete their initial service commitment at different career points depending on when they completed undergraduate pilot training (UPT), while other career milestones (e.g., promotion to O-6 or retirement) do not directly relate to UPT completion. To estimate the loss/affiliation rates for longer commitments, we use generalized boosted models (GBMs) to draw on the patterns among pilots who completed UPT later because of ordinary delays in the training pipeline or because they cross-trained from other career fields. GBMs use a statistical learning algorithm to assemble thousands of smaller pieces into a larger model that can approximate complex interactive and nonlinear relationships. They are extremely adept at fitting odd surfaces, such as the spikes in loss probability that occur when pilots separate or are eligible for retirement.

---

[2] The Palace Chase program is a personnel management tool that allows for pilots who are committed to the RegAF to transfer to an RC and serve out their remaining time at a 2:1 payback rate. The TFSC concept essentially raises the commitment length to greater than 10 years while making it agnostic as to the component that the commitment applies to, i.e., a pilot could transfer to from the RegAF to either the Air Force Reserve or Air National Guard and serve out the remainder of their commitment at a 1:1 rate.

TFSC Model Results

The results consist of two model scenarios driven by different assumptions about new pilot production. The first set assumes that current production plans cannot change and examines the impact of the TFSC policy on the pilot inventory compared with a baseline with no policy changes. Planned pilot production levels for this scenario were provided by the Air Force Directorate of Training and Readiness (AF/A3T). The second set allows the TFSC model to reallocate production across communities and components, subject to limits that were also provided by AF/A3T, if doing so helps to meet policy goals.

Under Planned Production, a Total Force Service Commitment Policy Reduces, but Does Not Eliminate, Shortages

Four results emerge from the analysis of planned production levels: (1) Most future shortages occur in the fighter pilot community, (2) TFSC policies cannot close the fighter pilot gap, (3) a combination of retention improvements and a modified Palace Chase program prevents mobility pilot shortages, and (4) overall, a TFSC policy reduces Total Force shortages but sacrifices RC health for improvements in RegAF health.

Figure S.1 shows the annual shortages for the RegAF (top panel) and RC (bottom panel) separately by flying community from FY17 through FY40. As the figure indicates, near-term RegAF shortages primarily exist in the fighter pilot community, but shortages also arise in the mobility pilot community starting in FY29. The RCs have enduring shortages in several pilot communities, but the majority of their unmet requirements are also in the fighter pilot community.

Figure S.1. Annual Shortages for the Regular Air Force (Top Panel) and Reserve Components (Bottom Panel) in Baseline Scenario with 10-Year Commitments and No Palace Chase Transfers

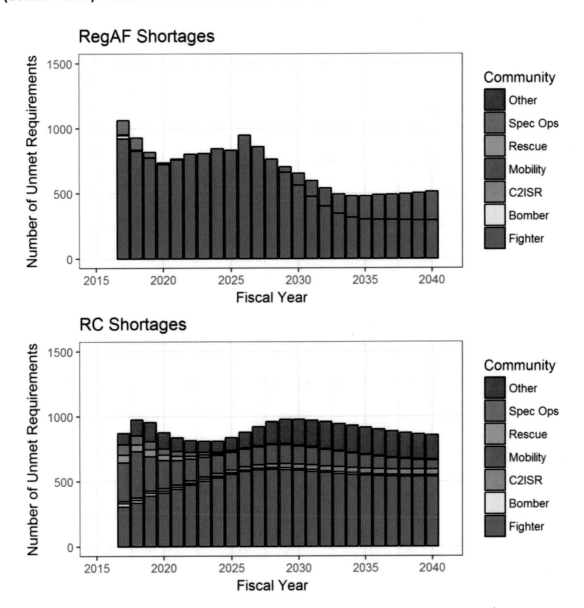

SOURCE: Authors' calculations from model results.
NOTES: "Other" community includes pilots in 11E, 11K, and 11G specialties. C2ISR (command, control, intelligence, surveillance, and reconnaissance) includes pilots in the 11R specialty.

Figure S.2 illustrates the effect of the TFSC policy on these shortages by comparing total numbers of unmet requirements for the current baseline policies (black dashed line) with the top of the bars generated with a TFSC policy requiring an 11-year commitment. In this scenario, the TFSC policy mitigates, but does not solve, Total Force shortages. Compared with the baseline case, the projections for a TFSC scenario with an 11-year commitment show close to a 50 percent reduction in unmet requirements by FY40. Further, the combination of better retention and additional flexibility from the modified Palace Chase program addresses the needs of all communities except fighter pilots.

Figure S.2. Annual Total Force Pilot Shortages Under Total Force Service Commitment of 11 Years Compared with Baseline Totals

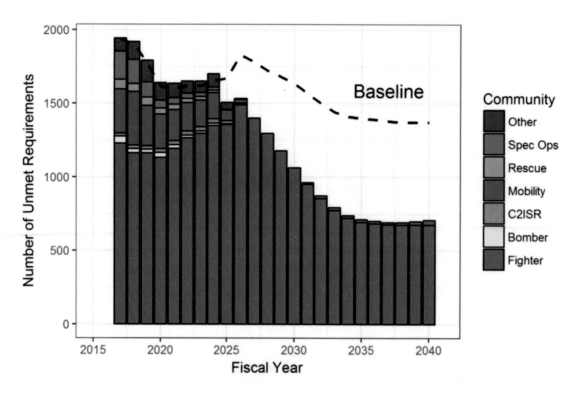

SOURCE: Authors' calculations from model results.
NOTES: "Other" community includes pilots in 11E, 11K, and 11G specialties. C2ISR includes pilots in the 11R specialty.

The results under lengthier commitments are qualitatively similar to the case of the 11-year TFSC—significant fighter pilot shortages remain when the TFSC requires 12, 13, or even 15 years of service. The main reason the TFSC policy has limited influence offsetting the shortage of fighter pilots is that the gains from improved retention are partly offset by the reduction in affiliations to the RCs. All TFSC scenarios result in significant steady-state improvements in *RegAF* health, but successively longer service commitments worsen *RC* shortages (especially in the Air Force Reserve, which depends heavily on affiliations for annual pilot gains). In theory, the Palace Chase path exists to compensate the RCs for decreased affiliations that result from the policy change (relative to the status quo). Yet, while significant RegAF shortages exist, the model opts to minimize Palace Chase transfers to avoid worsening those shortages. Thus, planned production levels are insufficient to meet the needs of all components, even if longer service commitments substantially improved retention.

Reallocated Production Meets Requirements Without Increased Commitment Length

In the previous results, the production of new pilots follows the planned levels in perpetuity, regardless of the health of each pilot community. Given that policymakers understand that fighter pilot health requires higher levels of production in the near and medium terms, we created a variant of the TFSC model that has some flexibility in setting community-specific production levels if different production levels help meet the model's goal of matching inventories to requirements. The following list enumerates the specific limitations that guide production decisions in the model. We developed these limitations cooperatively with action officers to ensure production decisions were realistic (see Chapter Four for more details):

- Total Force production cannot exceed the planned total in each year through FY20, and is capped at 1,350 per year thereafter.
- Pilot-community-specific production cannot be less than 90 percent of the planned level.
- RegAF production cannot exceed theoretical limitations for each pilot community (provided by AF/A3TF) that steadily increase over time. For example, fighter pilot production builds from 284 in FY17 to 352 in FY24, and mobility pilot production builds from 269 to 490 in the same period.
- RC production cannot exceed planned levels.
- After the buildup through FY24, annual production in each community cannot deviate from the previous year by more than 3 percent, to ensure stability over time.

This phase of the analysis yielded three results: (1) Reallocated production levels are close to planned levels, with a reallocation toward higher fighter pilot production, (2) additional capacity to produce fighter pilots is enough to end shortages without increasing commitment length (but does not address the fighter pilot absorption issue), and (3) reallocated production with a 10-year commitment meets all requirements before FY40.

Figure S.3 compares the planned production levels that underlie the previous results with the reallocated production levels under a TFSC of 10 years. The model reallocates production to the fighter and mobility pilot communities in anticipation of shortages, while reducing pilot production in other areas where planned production is higher than needed for sustainment under the loss rates assumed. This pattern is consistent across different TFSC lengths, except that fighter and mobility pilot production decreases slightly with longer service commitments because fewer new pilots are needed to replace losses.

Figure S.3. Average Annual Regular Air Force Production Under Total Force Service Commitment of 10 Years: Planned Versus Reallocated Scenarios

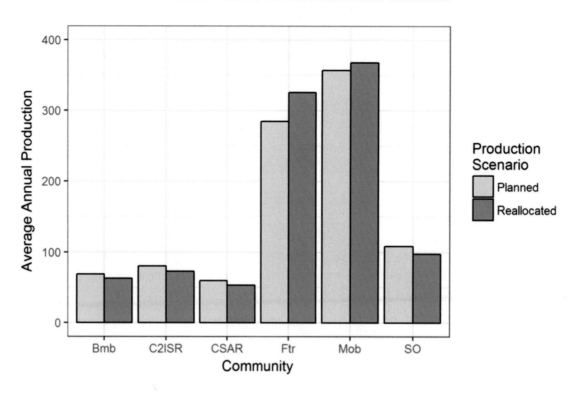

SOURCE: Authors' calculations from model results.
NOTE: The reallocated production scenario allows Palace Chase transfers, because the availability of Palace Chase affects production and allows more RC requirements to be met. Bmb = bomber; C2ISR = command and control, intelligence, surveillance, and reconnaissance; CSAR = combat search and rescue; Ftr = fighter; Mob = mobility; SO = special operations.

If production changes such as those summarized in Figure S.3 were feasible, they would change the dynamics of the TFSC policy in the fighter pilot community. Figure S.4 illustrates the new dynamics by showing fighter pilot inventory projections for the baseline scenario (i.e., planned production) and several scenarios involving reallocated production levels. For the RegAF (shown in the top panel of the figure), the ability to reallocate production within the prescribed limits enables the model to bridge the gap between inventory and requirements. The only difference between the reallocated scenarios is the timeline associated with meeting all requirements. However, the increased production alone only slightly benefits the RCs relative to the baseline, because affiliations alone do not provide enough fighter pilots to offset RC shortages. Only the combination of increased RegAF production and additional Palace Chase transfers to the RCs can enable the Total Force fighter pilot inventory to meet requirements.

Furthermore, the results under reallocated production indicate that longer service commitments produce only minimal inventory improvements if increases in fighter production are possible. The main reason for this result is that increases in service commitment length apply only to new cohorts, and, therefore, it takes at least 10 years before the new cohorts change the inventory relative to what it would have been under the current commitment length. By the time these effects begin to materialize in the RegAF, the production increases have already raised inventory levels close to requirements. Rather than changing the inventory trajectory, a consistent result has been that increased service commitment lengths mostly affect the steady-state production level once the inventory has reached healthy levels.

Figure S.4. Fighter Pilot Requirements (Red Line) Versus Inventory (Blue Line) for the Regular Air Force (Top Panel) and Reserve Components (Bottom Panel)

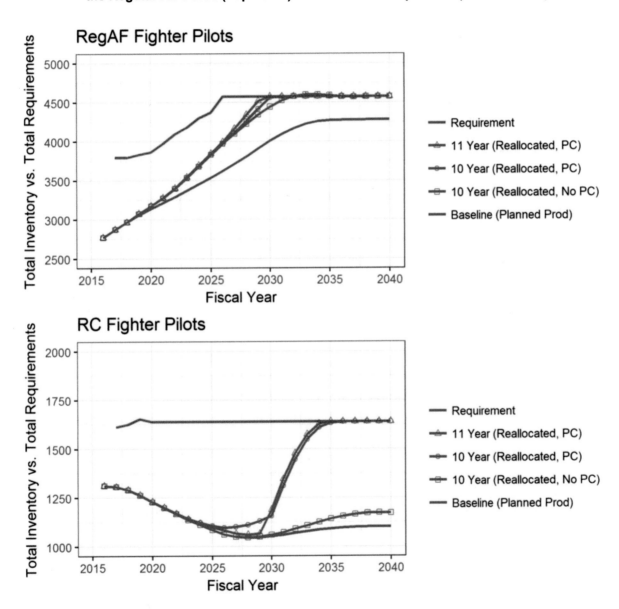

SOURCE: Authors' calculations from model results.
NOTE: Baseline scenario assumes a 10-year commitment and does not allow Palace Chase transfers. PC = Palace Chase.

Total Force Service Commitment Policy Conclusions

These results indicate that whether a TFSC policy could contribute to a solution to the aircrew crisis depends on multiple factors. The effectiveness of a TFSC policy depends on the community or component that has the shortage, as well as the expected flexibility in transfers and affiliations. The model results show that a TFSC policy could partially mitigate shortages if production plans are unalterable but that the benefits of longer service commitments become less important if certain production adjustments are possible. In addition to the specific results presented above, we provide the following general conclusions to guide decisionmaking in this area:

- **Whether a TFSC policy can bring inventories into alignment hinges on the size of retention gains relative to shortages.** Without production changes, the success of a TFSC policy requires the policy change to retain enough additional pilots in each component and community to cover shortfalls.
- **Production adjustments are necessary to fully address long-run shortages.** Under the assumptions of this analysis, only scenarios that allowed for increased production in key areas were capable of fully addressing pilot shortages.
- **The timing and size of TFSC impacts make the policy unlikely to play a major role in addressing the aircrew crisis.** We found the TFSC policy to be of limited effectiveness in reducing shortfalls, because the net increase in the long-run fighter inventory was modest, and because policy impacts do not occur until new cohorts reach the point where they would have completed their initial service commitment under existing policy. By contrast, production changes begin to affect the inventory as soon as new pilots arrive.
- **Persistent shortages create a trade-off between RegAF and RC health.** When a shortage existed in both the RegAF and the RC (i.e., in the fighter community), there was a tendency for the model to keep as many pilots in the RegAF as possible to meet RegAF requirements. With low Palace Chase utilization due to RegAF demand, higher TFSCs tended to starve the RCs of affiliations, which exacerbated shortages.
- **Affiliation flexibility significantly affects RC shortfalls.** The RC mobility community has historically accepted pilots from multiple RegAF communities, which gave the model more flexibility in using Palace Chase to align Total Force inventories and requirements. As a result, the TFSC policy was more successful in addressing mobility shortfalls than fighter shortfalls.
- **Other potential limitations of a TFSC policy could partly offset inventory improvements.** This analysis does not account for some potential costs of the TFSC policy, such as the possible impact of longer service commitments on the availability and quality of future recruits. Before implementing a TFSC policy, such costs and other limitations discussed above (e.g., absorption) should be investigated and given due consideration.

Acknowledgments

We are grateful to a number of Air Force personnel who have assisted in this study. Col Anthony Angello (Reserve Advisor to HAF/A3), Col Terry Frady (Katt) (AF/A3T), Col C. J. Will (ANG Advisor to HAF/A3), Emi Izawa (AF/A1P), and Lt Col Jeff Clark (AF/A3TF) served as our action officers and points of contact and were instrumental in providing us with data, context, and insights into Total Force pilot management.

We would like to thank Ray Conley, Director of the Manpower, Personnel, and Training Program in RAND Project AIR FORCE, for his direction and support of this research. We also thank our RAND colleague and associate director of the Manpower, Personnel, and Training Program, Kirsten Keller, for a helpful review of the document that further strengthened our work and results. Moreover, we are grateful for the thoughtful comments of our reviewers, Bart Bennett and Edward Chan, which significantly improved this report.

Abbreviations

ADSC	active duty service commitment
AF/A3T	Air Force Directorate of Training and Readiness
AF/A3TF	Air Force Total Force Aircrew Management office
AFI	Air Force Instruction
AFR	Air Force Reserve
ANG	Air National Guard
C2ISR	command, control, intelligence, surveillance, and reconnaissance
CYOS	commissioned years of service
FY	fiscal year
GBM	generalized boosted model
RC	reserve component
RegAF	Regular Air Force
RPA	remotely piloted aircraft
RSC	reserve service commitment
TARS	total active rated service
TFAM	Total Force Aircrew Management
TFBL	Total Force Blue Line
TFSC	Total Force service commitment
TRRS	total reserve rated service
UPT	undergraduate pilot training
YORE	years of retirement eligibility
YOSE	years of separation eligibility

Chapter 1. Introduction

The Air Force faces a shortage of pilots and career enlisted aviators that senior leaders have described as an "aircrew crisis." In March 2017, the Air Force Deputy Chief of Staff for Manpower, Personnel, and Services testified before Congress that the Total Force shortage at the end of fiscal year (FY) 2016 was 1,555 pilots, most of whom resided in the fighter community (Grosso, 2017). This crisis occurs at a particularly difficult time, because efforts to reduce shortages will face headwinds in the form of surging major airline hiring. Research has shown that increases in major airline hiring correlate with higher pilot attrition (McGee, 2015; Sweeney, 2015). While the Air Force has occasionally faced temporary spikes in major airline demand that draw more pilots out of the Regular Air Force (RegAF), there is no historical precedent for the sustained level of demand that is projected in the years to come (McGee, 2015). Recent data cited in the March 2017 testimony suggest that the major airline hiring environment is turning out to be worse for the Air Force than projected, with more pilots hired and faster increases in airline compensation (Grosso, 2017). Furthermore, leaders have keyed in on additional quality-of-life issues, such as the burden of additional duties and maintaining work-life balance, that could decrease pilots' attachment to the Air Force, all else being equal.

Reducing the pilot shortage simply requires either an increase in the pilot inventory or a reduction in pilot requirements. For the latter, Air Force policymakers are moving to reduce requirements for pilots outside of operational units, as was recommended in Robbert et al. (2015). Unlike rearranging requirements, increasing the pilot inventory is a multifaceted problem, requiring attention to production capacity at all points in the training pipeline, incorporating new pilots into operational units and affording them sufficient flying time to gain experience (known as *absorption*), and retention of experienced pilots once they complete their initial service commitments. In past shortages, absorption has actually been the most acute issue (Taylor, Moore, and Roll, 2000), because operational units cannot function with too many inexperienced pilots and not enough flying hours to go around (Robbert et al., 2015). Some fear that reductions in the number of operational units since the 1991 Gulf War have left the Air Force in a position where larger numbers of pilots headed for fighter aircraft after undergraduate pilot training (UPT) would face an absorption bottleneck (Skowronski, 2016). To resolve this problem, Air Force leaders are also considering options that increase absorption as well as production, such as using reserve component (RC) units to help absorb new RegAF pilots (Grosso, 2017)—a sort of "win-win" scenario that also helps address reserve shortages while simultaneously boosting RegAF absorption.

In addition to reducing requirements and increasing production and absorption capacity, policymakers also hope to increase retention of experienced pilots by offering a combination of compensation increases and quality-of-life changes. However, one additional retention tool implicit in these discussions is the length of the initial service commitment that pilots receive after completing UPT. The current active duty service commitment (ADSC) attached to UPT is 10 years, which has been in place since FY99. Air Force regulations highlight that a key purpose of ADSCs is to ensure that the Air Force receives an "appropriate return for their investment" (Air Force Instruction [AFI] 36-2107, 2012). Thus, the service commitment functions as a retention guarantee to prevent the amount of rated service provided after UPT completion from falling to unacceptable levels. If changes in the civilian pilot labor market have upended the equilibrium retention levels, perhaps adjustments in the service commitments are needed to increase retention and the Air Force's return on investment.

An additional consideration in improving pilot retention is the impact on the RCs—the Air Force Reserve (AFR) and Air National Guard (ANG). RC units rely mainly on prior service RegAF pilots who separate and affiliate, so improvements in RegAF retention could result in several years of fewer affiliations, further exacerbating RC shortages. For this reason, policymakers have discussed increased service commitments coupled with additional paths of cross-flow between the RegAF and the RCs (Skowronski, 2016).

Examining a Total Force Service Commitment Policy

In light of these challenges, the Total Force Aircrew Management (TFAM) office (AF/A3TF) within the Directorate of Training and Readiness (AF/A3T) asked RAND to evaluate whether a Total Force service commitment (TFSC) policy with increased service commitments could decrease the pilot shortage. Such a policy would replace the current ADSC and reserve service commitment (RSC) of 10 years with a TFSC greater than 10 years in duration. The TFSC policy features an expansion and modification of the Palace Chase program—which AFI 36-3205 describes as "an early release program which allows active Air Force officers and enlisted members to request to transfer from active military status to an Air Reserve Component," with a key provision stipulating that the member "continue in the Selected Reserve for a period of not less than two times the length of the remaining ADSC" (AFI 36-3205, 2009). The concept of a TFSC potentially increases the flow of pilots from the RegAF to the RCs while stripping the two-to-one payback rate and only requiring pilots to serve out the initial agreed-upon length in total.

The Palace Chase expansion and modification would serve two purposes. First, it would provide a lever to offset the decrease in affiliations caused by improved retention under a lengthier service commitment. Second, a longer service commitment might be more palatable to new recruits if it were bundled with the possibility of serving part of the additional time in an RC.

Provided that the Air Force can meet its production goals, a longer commitment would inherently increase the pilot inventory over time; however, information is lacking on the magnitude and timing of the improvement, and on the likely effect on each individual

2

component. This report fills these research gaps by adapting RAND's Total Force Blue Line model (Terry et al., forthcoming) to simulate the steady-state impact of a TFSC policy across the Total Force pilot community. TFBL is a career field planning model that projects future numbers of pilots under different policy scenarios, which can then be compared with planned requirements for an assessment of career field health.

Organization of This Report

Chapter Two of this report summarizes how a TFSC policy would change the inventory flow and create avenues for raising inventory levels, while Chapter Three discusses our method for creating plausible retention and affiliation patterns by increasing the service commitment length. Chapter Four shows whether a TFSC policy can reduce the Total Force pilot shortages, and Chapter Five provides concluding thoughts on the implications of these results.

Chapter 2. The Impact of a Total Force Service Commitment Policy on Inventory Flows

Moving from the current construct of 10-year, component-specific service commitments to a TFSC policy with a longer commitment would change the way many pilots move within the Total Force. Because the effect of the proposed policy is a combination of many factors and limitations, it is beneficial to build a workforce model to test hypotheses and inform decisionmakers. RAND's Total Force Blue Line (TFBL) model is a tool that RAND researchers developed to help inform personnel managers about whether future numbers of rated officers (i.e., *inventories*) will match rated requirements under different production and retention scenarios. For the research presented here, we began with the TFBL and made adjustments to its inputs and structure to allow for the key components of the TFSC policy—increased commitment length and an expanded Palace Chase Program.[1] This chapter reviews the fundamentals of the TFBL model, describes the necessary modifications for the current application, and discusses how the changes could potentially affect future pilot shortages. Further technical details of the TFBL model are available in Harrington et al. (2016), Terry et al. (2017), and Terry et al. (forthcoming). Appendix A contains a technical formulation of the modified model.

Inventory Flow in the Total Force Blue Line Model

RAND researchers originally developed TFBL to provide the capability of understanding how the movement of personnel across components, such as when pilots leave the RegAF and subsequently join (or "affiliate to") either the AFR or the ANG, might affect Total Force health. These cross-component movements are difficult to predict, because they must reconcile both the supply side (the population of qualified pilots who leave the RegAF and are willing to affiliate) and the demand side (vacancies in the RCs). The TFBL model approaches this question as an optimization problem to be solved by determining the number of affiliations that match the RC inventory as closely as possible to the number of RC rated requirements, with affiliations capped according to historical affiliation rates. However, TFBL is flexible enough that other key

---

[1] As noted in Chapter One, the Palace Chase program is a personnel management tool that allows for pilots who are committed to the RegAF to transfer to the RC and serve out their remaining time at a 2:1 payback rate. The TFSC concept essentially raises the commitment length to greater than ten years while making it agnostic as to the component that the commitment applies to, i.e., a pilot could transfer to from the RegAF to either the AFR or ANG and serve out the remainder of their commitment at a 1:1 rate.

4

variables, such as production levels, can also be optimally determined to match inventories to requirements.

Beyond its optimization aspects, the essential function of TFBL determines future inventories by subtracting expected losses and adding in expected gains to the population in each component and flying community broken out by commissioned years of service (CYOS) and FY. Researchers can then determine how different policies might affect future losses or gains, and plug new parameters into TFBL to assess the effect on the future manning outlook.[2] Gains and losses occur as new pilots complete UPT, as existing pilots leave, when pilots affiliate to an RC after leaving the RegAF, or when pilots transfer (or cross-flow) to a different community. Each of these forces is guided by model inputs that are either data-driven or based on Air Force planning assumptions.

Projected Inventories Result from Applying Inventory Flows to Current Manning Levels

The initial pilot inventory in the TFBL model is the number of personnel in each component (RegAF, AFR, or ANG), community (fighter pilot, bomber pilot, etc.), and CYOS, and these numbers come from the most recent end-of-FY snapshot of personnel data. The TFBL model calculates future inventory levels by applying predicted workforce trends to the starting inventory, while also adding in newly produced pilots. The adding and subtracting of personnel from each category over time are often referred to as the inventory *flows* (Figure 2.1). As the model steps through time, incrementing by one FY, all pilots who remain in the Air Force "age" into the next CYOS and FY. The TFBL model automatically subtracts annual losses from each inventory category and includes the capability to subtract any transfers that are planned to take place.[3] As departing pilots are removed from each category, newly produced pilots, affiliations (taken as a subset of the RegAF losses), and transfers are added to the gaining components and communities to arrive at the subsequent year's inventory levels. Each flow affecting the inventory requires guidance from a model input that is either calculated from historical data (such as loss or affiliation rates) or given as a planning assumption (such as production).

---

[2] We use the terms *manning* and *manning health* to refer to the degree to which there are enough pilots available to meet existing and projected job requirements.

[3] For example, Terry et al. (forthcoming) uses such transfers to capture planned, temporary rotations of 11X pilots to fill Remotely Piloted Aircraft pilot duties. The transfer flow is generic, and could be used for planned rotations of pilots to/from any desired inventory category.

Figure 2.1. Illustration of Inventory Flows in the Total Force Blue Line Model

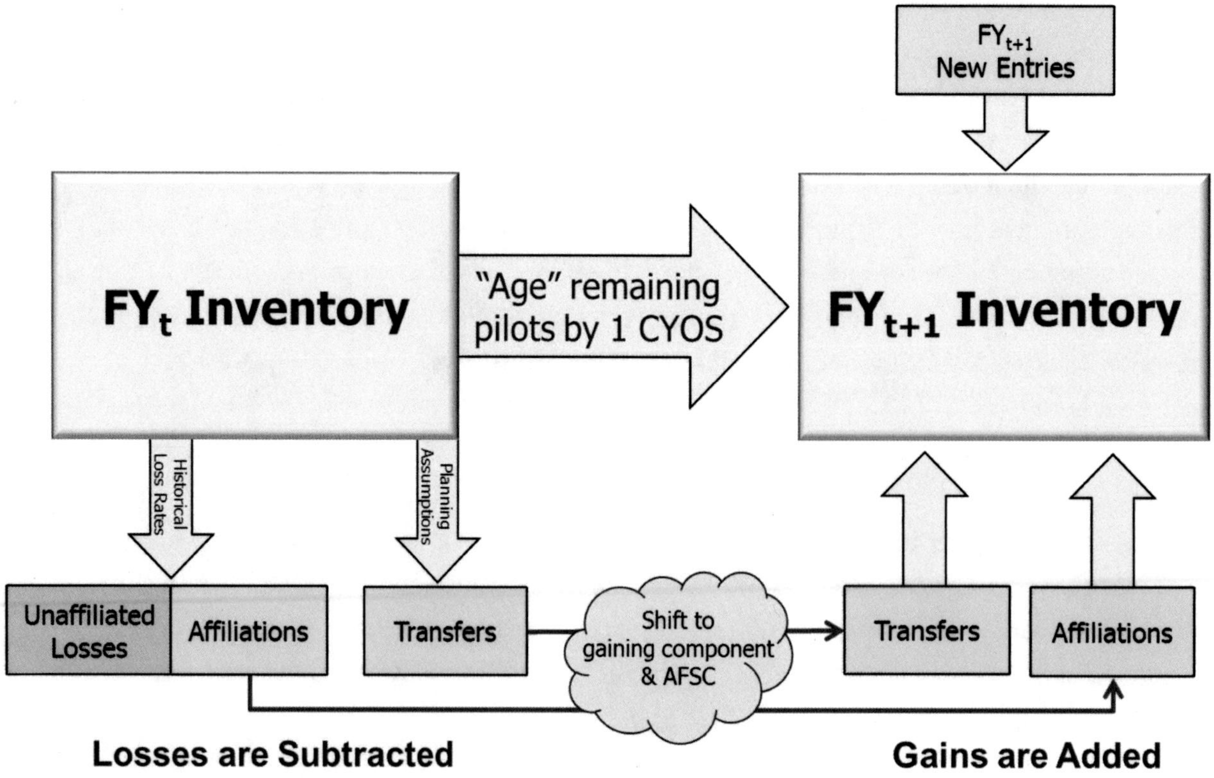

NOTE: All pilots who remain within the Total Force, including those who affiliate or transfer, age into the next CYOS with each FY.

Inventory Flows Can Be Preprogrammed or Goal-Seeking

There are two ways that the TFBL model determines the flows that affect future inventories. First, the flows can proceed automatically each year based on estimates of recent trends or planning assumptions. For example, the TFBL model determines losses by applying a loss rate that the user has specified for each inventory category, and the typical input for these loss rates are historical percentages calculated from recent data. Production can also be fixed at planned levels to see whether the production plans result in long-run health under a given retention pattern. An alternative capability of the TFBL model is that it can determine the optimum flow for each inventory category in order to achieve a goal. In place of the rote application of historical trends, the TFBL model can use the historical trends as a guide while determining inventory flows that best achieve policy aims, as expressed by an overall objective function. The canonical set of force management goals that prior work has considered include matching inventories to requirements as closely as possible, exercising economy in production, and matching the historical pattern of affiliations as closely as possible. In practice, the TFBL objective function considers these goals by attempting to minimize the sum of unmet requirements, unassigned personnel, newly produced pilots, and deviations from the historical spread of affiliations across components and communities. An example of how we employ this optimum-flow capability is when we later compare results under planned production with results for which the model is permitted to reallocate production capacity to reduce shortages.

Regardless of which modeling approach is used (fixed inputs with automatically calculated flows, or optimizing flows), the accuracy of the inventory flows rests on the assumed guidelines from recent data. However, workforce trends in the future are likely to deviate from those assumed in the model, especially over long periods of time. It is most appropriate, then, to view the TFBL model and similar techniques as tools that help identify the best long-term strategy for the current situation (Robbert et al., 2015). In the case of the TFSC policy, the goal is to use a variant of the TFBL model to learn about the inventory effects of longer service commitments under a TFSC policy rather than to generate the closest-possible prediction of future inventory levels.

Total Force Service Commitment Alterations to the Total Force Blue Line Model

Beginning with the TFBL model as a template for assessing whether different pieces of the Total Force are postured to meet future requirements, we built in some additional structure to capture the key components of the TFSC policy, forming a TFBL variant that we call the "TFSC model." This section describes the model alterations that were necessary to carry out the analysis, along with the goals behind some of the modeling decisions. A technical formulation of the TFSC model can be found in Appendix A.

The TFSC Model Requires Adjusted Loss and Affiliation Behavior to Capture the Effect of Longer Commitments

First, examining the effect of a TFSC policy on steady-state inventory levels calls for adjusted loss and affiliation patterns that reflect the increased service commitment length. The baseline TFBL model captures loss behavior by applying historical annual loss rates to each group of pilots by CYOS, while allowing a percentage of the losses to affiliate to the RC according to historical affiliation rates by CYOS. Both sets of rates need to be adjusted for scenarios involving longer service commitments (our method for adjusting these rates is detailed in Chapter Three). For instance, the RegAF has distinct retention patterns reflecting key career points at which separation and retirement decisions can be made, such as completion of the initial, 10-year ADSC. An increase in service commitment length, then, would shift the point in time when pilots can decide to separate to later in the career, when they are closer to the traditional 20-year retirement point. Pilots making retention decisions later could have different likelihoods of leaving and/or affiliating, for which the TFSC model must account.

The TFSC Model Requires an Explicit Palace Chase Path from the Regular Air Force to the Reserve Components

In addition to modified loss and affiliation rates that reflect longer service commitments, assessing a TFSC policy also requires a second modification: an explicit Palace Chase path to the RCs. We enabled this path in the TFSC model by allowing pilots in the RegAF to move across different "populations" over time (Figure 2.2). When pilots first enter the RegAF, they must serve a minimum amount of time before becoming eligible for Palace Chase (we denote this initial group as the "Pre-window" population, because they are not yet in the eligibility window for Palace Chase). After serving the minimum amount of time (eight years in Figure 2.2), pilots move into the "window" population, where they remain until the completion of the TFSC. Pilots in the window population are available to transfer into the RC if it helps to meet the policy goals underlying the model (i.e., the model determines the optimal set of Palace Chase transfers each year). Upon completion of the TFSC, pilots move to the "post-SC" population, where they can no longer move to the RC through a Palace Chase transfer but are still able to leave the RegAF and affiliate according to the normal inventory flows.

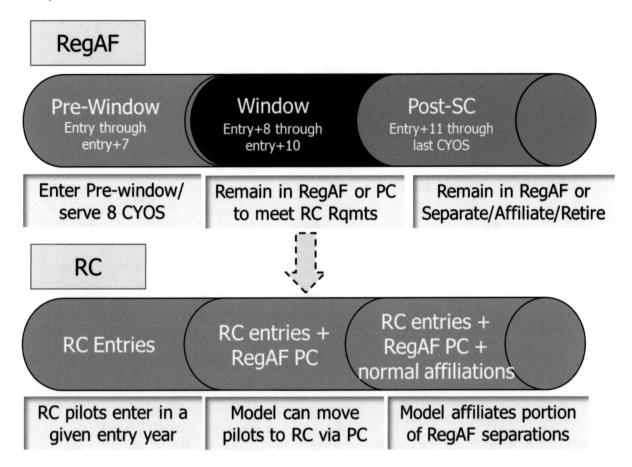

Figure 2.2. Inventory Flow Across Populations in TFSC Model
(11-Year Service Commitment in Which Palace Chase Window Opens After Eight Years)

NOTE: The *PC* abbreviation refers to Palace Chase transfers. RC entries are pilots who begin their careers in the RC, in contrast to those who begin in the AC and transfer or affiliate. *Post-SC* refers to pilots who have completed their initial service commitments.

The flows illustrated in Figure 2.2 highlight another major change from the TFBL model, which is that the model must track inventory levels by entry year in addition to CYOS to ensure correct transition across populations. This modification greatly increases the scale of the problem (and computational difficulty), but it also improves the quality of the analysis because it allows the model to differentiate between the pilots who are eligible for Palace Chase from those who are not, within a given CYOS. Furthermore, the method for estimating loss rates (detailed in Chapter Three) allows for a custom loss profile for each entry year. Thus, the model captures, as closely as possible, the interplay between service commitment length, expected loss patterns, and Palace Chase eligibility.

Goals Guiding TFSC Model Decisions

Many inventory flows in the TFSC model proceed automatically according to pre-established parameters (e.g., loss rates). By contrast, the model calculates affiliations, Palace Chase transfers, and production levels (in certain scenarios) according to an overarching function expressing the policy goals. This tactic is useful in complex models, where there is a clear sense of the objective but there are too many possible paths to investigate manually. Specifically, the TFSC model proceeds according to the following goals:[4]

- **Meet as many requirements as possible:** Minimize requirements that cannot be filled with a qualified pilot in a given component/community.[5]
- **Minimize overages**: Minimize excess pilots who cannot be matched to an open requirement in a given component/community.
- **Minimize production:** Produce the fewest number of pilots possible while meeting other goals.
- **Follow historical affiliation norms:** Match historical affiliation patterns as closely as possible when affiliating or transferring pilots from the RegAF to the RCs.
- **Use Palace Chase as a last resort:** Minimize the use of Palace Chase transfers while meeting other goals.

Except for minimizing Palace Chase transfers, the model goals receive equal weight. This means that the model views one unmet requirement the same as one excess pilot, a one-pilot increase in production, and a one-pilot deviation from the historical affiliation norm. In the formulation presented in this report, Palace Chase transfers receive an additional penalty, which means the model will use the program only if it helps to save multiple units across the other goals. This penalty serves to ensure that Palace Chase transfers are a last resort and brings the model's decision process more in line with how career field planners would operate.[6]

To understand the interplay among these goals, it might be helpful to consider, as an example, how the model would cope with a shortage of fighter pilots in the RCs in the case where production is fixed at planned levels. To address the shortage, the model would first look to the pool of RegAF losses and affiliate as many as possible according to historical affiliation paths and rates. If shortages remain, it would then look to move eligible pilots from the RegAF via Palace Chase along the same affiliation paths, unless doing so would undermine other goals and outweigh the potential gain. If there is a shortage in the RegAF as well, it would move pilots

---

[4] The first four goals are identical to those of the TFBL model. In practice, the first two goals tend to be more dominant in the objective function, because overages and shortages can persist through time, whereas production, affiliations, and Palace Chase transfers impose a one-time cost at the point where they occur.

[5] *Qualified* in this context represents general limitations, such as only fighter pilots can fill fighter pilot requirements, only bomber pilots can fill bomber pilot requirements, etc. We note that the model has the capability to have more-strict definitions of *qualified*.

[6] The numeric penalty that the model assigns to a Palace Chase transfer is 5. We tested different penalties and found that this value promoted the right model behavior. This penalty is not so high that the model will leave RC requirements unmet when RegAF pilots are available, but the model still uses the program as a last resort after maxing out RC production and affiliations. After discussions with our action officers, we also decided to place a lower bound on Palace Chase transfers each year, set at 2 percent of the window population in each community. This ensures a minimal amount of program use even in the presence of a RegAF shortage.

to the RCs only if such a movement could fill more requirements or fill requirements for a longer duration in the RCs than in the RegAF.[7] The interplay among these goals is complex, and, for this reason, part of the value in the approach is the increased understanding that comes with examining the model's decisions.

Avenues for a Total Force Service Commitment Policy to Improve Long-Term Manning Outlook

There are two ways in which the TFSC policy, as formulated here, could improve the Total Force manning outlook. The most obvious way is that it increases total active rated service (TARS, i.e., the average total rated service each pilot contributes to the RegAF) and total reserve rated service (TRRS, i.e., the average total rated service each pilot contributes to the RCs) by causing pilots to stay in their initial components longer, thereby delaying and/or reducing unaffiliated losses prior to retirement. A second way the TFSC policy could improve Total Force manning is by allowing surplus RegAF pilots who do not separate to transfer to RC communities in need. For these reasons, one would expect the effect of the TFSC policy on the Total Force inventory level to be positive.

However, decisionmakers also need information on the magnitude of this positive effect and whether the gains will be shared among all components and communities. The magnitude of potential inventory effects could be modest, as longer commitments primarily target retention at the point of initial service commitment completion, where affiliation rates are typically very high (e.g., 70–90 percent, according to Robbert et al., 2015). Therefore, the gains from holding onto those who would have separated from the RegAF without affiliating could be small compared with the decrease in affiliations to the RCs from increased RegAF retention. Additionally, we programmed the model to determine Palace Chase utilization according to the policy goal of meeting requirements as closely as possible, which potentially creates an incentive for the model to underutilize Palace Chase in communities where RegAF manning is poor. For these reasons, a full examination of the inventory model is a useful exercise to illuminate the trade-offs that policymakers might face in adopting a TFSC policy.

---

[7] Historical retention rates show that the RCs have better retention, in that officers in the RCs stay longer in duration than they do in the RegAF. Thus, a Palace Chase transfer can result in the officer filling a requirement for more years in the RCs than the RegAF. One of the reasons we put an additional penalty on Palace Chase transfers was to prevent the model from using Palace Chase to increase the Total Force inventory simply by moving pilots out of the RegAF early in their careers.

Chapter 3. Loss and Affiliation Adjustments for Increased Service Commitment Length

This chapter summarizes our method for creating loss and affiliation patterns for what might be expected from RegAF and RC pilots under a lengthier service commitment. First, we describe the analytical data set and the concept of how we approached the problem, followed by a discussion of the estimation methods and examples of the results.

Recent Personnel Records Serve as the Data Source for This Analysis

To model loss and affiliation probability across the Total Force, we drew on a large dataset, spanning FY01 through FY16, of all manned-aircraft pilots in grades O-1 through O-5 across the three components in CYOS 0 to 30. The data files were drawn from end-of-FY master personnel extracts provided by the Air Force Personnel Center, with information on officers on active duty, as well as officers in the AFR or ANG.[1] The data contain information on the flying community and CYOS of each pilot in each FY.

Further, the analytical strategy described below also requires information on separation and retirement eligibility. The RegAF data include the dates associated with each pilot's current ADSCs, including the initial ADSC associated with UPT. However, there was no information on the RSC associated with UPT for RC pilots, so we assumed either an 8- or 10-year commitment based on when the RC pilots entered the data. This means that RC pilots who were fully qualified in the first year of data could not be used to inform estimates of loss behavior around the initial separation point. We assumed all pilots would become retirement eligible after 20 CYOS.

The primary outcomes the analysis examined are losses and affiliations. For RegAF pilots, a loss occurs when a pilot exits the O-1 through O-5 population in the subsequent period.[2] For RC pilots, we considered pilots lost if they exited the RC as a whole, but not if they transferred from AFR to ANG and vice versa. To determine when affiliations occurred, we took the pool of separated RegAF pilots and identified which pilots later turned up in the AFR or ANG. We treated affiliation to the ANG and affiliation to the AFR as separate outcomes.

---

[1] The data came from the BAE (file part b active extract), BRE (file part b reserve extract), and BGE (file part b guard extract), where *file part b* means the officer monthly snapshots provided by the Air Force Personnel Center.

[2] Thus, from the model's perspective, there are four kinds of losses that are considered a loss in the aggregate sense: separations, retirements, grounding/other losses, and promotions to O-6.

Concept for Loss and Affiliation Patterns Under Increased Commitment Length

A starting point for projecting losses in an inventory model is to use a straightforward loss rate, which is calculated as the number of pilots in each CYOS who leave in the current period (but were there in the previous period) divided by the total number of pilots who completed the previous period in that CYOS. The corresponding affiliation rate would then be the number of those departures who affiliate to the AFR or ANG divided by the total number of pilots who leave the RegAF. The service commitment length is implicitly contained in the loss rates, because they assume that the patterns (key retention decisions after completing commitments) in the previous data will continue.

Usually, accurately predicting retention profiles under never-before-seen circumstances first requires the detailed formulation of a model of retention behavior (see Mattock et al., 2016, for a recent example). With an accurate model of historical individual choices, one can proceed to feed new circumstances to the model to see how individual choices will likely change and the net effect of the new circumstances. The application of this method was beyond the scope of the current effort, so we sought an off-the-shelf method that could quickly manipulate the historical loss patterns into plausible loss and affiliation rates for the TFSC model.

While very little historical variation occurs in the length of service commitments, there is variation in the point in pilots' careers at which the initial service commitments are completed. This variation arises from the fact that service commitments are based on UPT completion, and pilots vary in the CYOS in which they complete UPT. Thus, we can use the loss behavior of pilots who completed UPT later in their careers to estimate plausible loss patterns for future pilots who are retained by an increased TFSC.

Instead of estimating loss probability as a direct function of CYOS, we modeled loss probability as a function of the time remaining in a pilot's initial service commitment (which we denote *years of separation eligibility*, or YOSE, following the convention established by prior research, such as Gates et al., 2013) and the time remaining until retirement (which we refer to as *years of retirement eligibility*, or YORE, following the convention established by Gates et al., 2013). Then, we determined the implications of service commitment length for these two values and used the model to predict the appropriate loss profile for each scenario. For example, consider a pilot in CYOS 10 who completed UPT in CYOS 2. Under existing policy, this pilot has two years of commitment remaining and 10 years remaining until retirement. To simulate a new loss profile under an 11-year TFSC, we would assign a new loss rate for CYOS 10 reflecting a pilot who had three years of commitment remaining, but still 10 years until retirement. The model would then use the historical information on pilots who completed UPT in CYOS 3 to predict the new loss rate. This concept generalizes readily to affiliation rates, which can also be characterized according to time until service commitment completion and time until retirement.

This concept assumes that future pilots who stay in because of a longer commitment length would behave similarly to pilots in the past who completed their commitments at the same point in time relative to retirement. This concept also assumes that those pilots who completed UPT in later CYOS (4, 5, or 6) will behave similarly to those pilots who completed UPT in the usual time frame, i.e., CYOS (1, 2, or 3). In reality, implementing a TFSC policy could change the retention dynamics in unpredictable ways. Other factors, such as the structure of retirement compensation and the characteristics of new accessions, could change as well. For these reasons, we use the word *plausible* to describe the estimates in this chapter, acknowledging that actual steady-state retention could look different.

Generalized Boosted Models Provide Methodology for Estimation of Loss and Affiliation Probabilities

Implementing the concept described in the previous section requires estimating a general regression function that predicts loss/affiliation probability using the YOSE/YORE values in the data. A function that fits the data appropriately can then be used to produce loss/affiliation profiles for different TFSC lengths by manipulating the YOSE/YORE inputs accordingly. However, traditional regression methods have several limitations that prevent their use in implementing this concept. First, a pilot's loss probability over the course of a career is unlikely to be approximated well by a smooth function, because it features long periods during which the loss probability is nearly zero (while under a service commitment or nearing retirement eligibility), with dramatic "spikes" in loss probability at distinct points (such as upon initial separation eligibility and upon retirement eligibility). Further, it would be ideal to adjust for factors such as component and community, but it is not necessarily more accurate to estimate rates separately by each category. For example, with small populations it could be more accurate to pool data across similar communities. An additional complication lies in the fact that we do not observe service commitment information in the data for some more-senior pilots who had already completed their initial commitments in the earliest waves. However, we cannot simply exclude these pilots from the analysis, because the data on senior pilots are essential for understanding late-career loss probabilities.

In light of these challenges, we turned to generalized boosted models (GBMs) to estimate loss probability and affiliation probability as a function of YOSE and YORE, as well as component and pilot community (Ridgeway, Madigan, and Richardson, 1999). GBMs use a statistical learning algorithm to assemble thousands of smaller pieces into a larger model that can approximate complex, interactive, and nonlinear relationships. They are extremely adept at fitting odd surfaces, such as the spikes in loss probability that occur when pilots become separation- or retirement-eligible. Additionally, they cope with the problem of small populations by incorporating strategies to prevent "over-fitting" the data. Further, they handle missing data seamlessly, so that the senior pilots with no separation information can be incorporated into the predictions (for a deeper description of the GBM method, see Ridgeway, 2007, or Chapter 10 of Hastie, Tibshirani, and Friedman, 2009).

Sample Loss and Affiliation Adjustment Results

Loss Rates for Increased Service Commitment Length

Using GBMs, we estimated a flexible model of loss probability as a function of YOSE, YORE, and flying community for RegAF separations, along with a separate model for RC separations that also included an indicator for ANG versus AFR.

First, Figure 3.1 illustrates the fit of the two GBMs by comparing their predictions with analogous historical loss patterns. Because a new TFSC policy would not affect pilots who are already in the inventory, these "legacy" pilots need a separate loss profile that continues to project historical trends with no increase in service commitment length. The 10-year commitment affected those *entering* UPT starting in FY99 (AFI 36-2107, 2012), so factoring in a rough two-year timeline for UPT implies that the first 15 CYOS of legacy pilots are from the 10-year service commitment era, while higher-CYOS pilots were subject to the previous 8-year commitment length. A sensible historical baseline for these legacy pilots, then, would be to draw on losses for the 10-year pilots in CYOS 1 through 15, coupled with the losses from earlier cohorts for later CYOS—CYOS 16 through 30. The predicted losses from the GBM require a commitment length and entry year as inputs (from which to derive YOSE and YORE), so we calculated legacy losses by estimating 10-year profiles for each entry year and doing a weighted average of these profiles according to historical entry year proportions. For both communities shown in the figure, the GBM predictions track very closely with the historical loss rates, even the irregular "zig-zags" beyond CYOS 20.

Figure 3.1. Regular Air Force Historical Compared with Predicted Losses for Legacy Mobility Pilots (Top Panel) and Fighter Pilots (Bottom Panel)

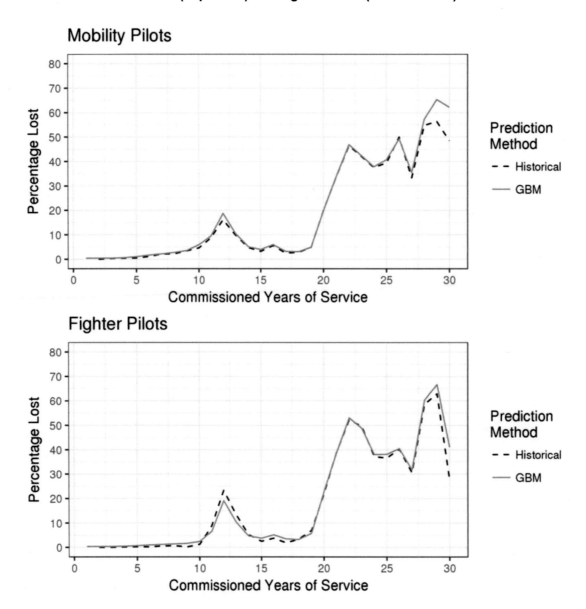

SOURCE: Authors' calculations from personnel data.
NOTE: Historical losses include only 10-year ADSC pilots for CYOS 1 through 15, and all other pilots in CYOS 16 through 30. GBM losses are a weighted average across entry CYOS for 10-year TFSC predictions.

Loss profiles for the RCs differ substantially from the RegAF patterns in Figure 3.1. The RegAF losses are low during the period in which all pilots are under ADSC, with a familiar "spike" in loss probability at the ADSC completion point. By contrast, RC loss profiles are relatively flat for most CYOS before increasing rapidly at the point of retirement eligibility (Figure 3.2). This pattern is consistent for both AFR and ANG (Robbert et al., 2015, Appendix B) and did not differ appreciably when we tried to account for whether pilots entered directly into an RC rather than first serving in the RegAF or separating and affiliating. For inventory

16

models in general, the primary concern is whether the losses accurately represent the recent trends. However, the key implication for this research is that the losses do not significantly change at the RSC completion point, which means predicted losses will not change substantially when simulating the effect of a higher TFSC.

Figure 3.2. Air Force Reserve Historical Compared with Predicted Losses for Legacy Mobility Pilots (Top Panel) and Fighter Pilots (Bottom Panel)

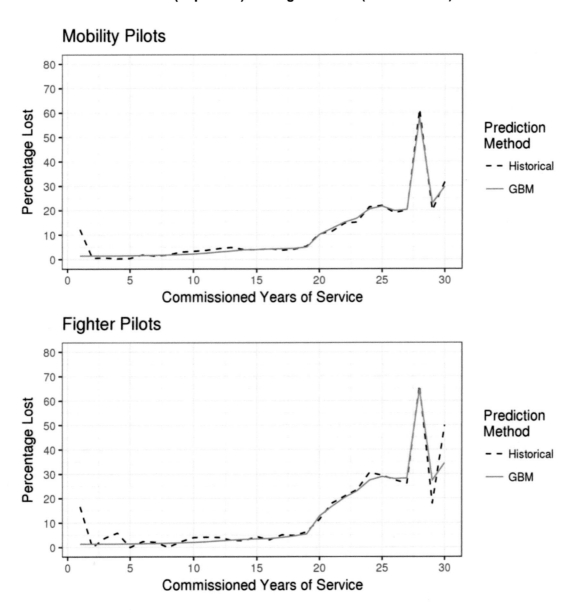

SOURCE: Authors' calculations from personnel data.
NOTE: Historical losses include all AFR pilots in the panel. GBM losses are a weighted average across entry CYOS for 10-year TFSC predictions.

Given that the GBMs adequately fit the historical patterns under commitment lengths of 10 years, we can now illustrate how the model adjusts these loss profiles for increases in the service commitment length. Figure 3.3 shows the effect of longer service commitments on cumulative retention for RegAF mobility pilots who begin their careers in CYOS 2 (top panel) and the corresponding picture for AFR mobility pilots (bottom panel). First, the RegAF cumulative retention curves reflect both a delay and a reduction in losses. Longer service commitments push back the initial point of separation eligibility, thus delaying the first significant drop-off in retention associated with ADSC completion. Higher TFSC lengths also shrink the magnitude of the retention dip at the ADSC completion point, reflecting the fact that pilots who complete their initial service commitments closer to retirement separate at lower rates. The end result is that cumulative retention at 19 CYOS (right before promotions to O-6 and retirements rapidly winnow the population) spans from 41 percent for a 10-year TFSC to 64 percent for a 15-year TFSC. This provides a wide range of retention levels with which to assess the impact on pilot inventories.

Figure 3.3. Cumulative Percentage Retained for Regular Air Force Mobility Pilots (Top Panel) and Air Force Reserve Mobility Pilots (Bottom Panel) for Varying Total Force Service Commitment Lengths

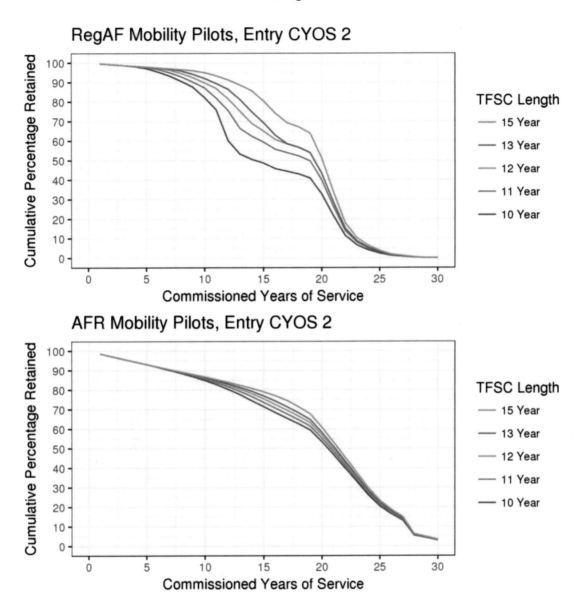

SOURCE: Authors' calculations from personnel data.

The bottom panel of Figure 3.3 shows that increased TFSC lengths do not affect RC retention as much, because of the weak relationship between RSC completion and loss probability. Still, the curves show that the method predicts slight improvements in RC retention with each successive increase in service commitment length.

The example losses in Figures 3.1 through 3.3 reflect a small subset of the actual loss rates inputted in the TFSC model. The GBM algorithm makes slight adjustments to the loss rates depending on the patterns in a pilot's component, flying community, and CYOS of entry, leading to a total of 161 distinct sets of loss rates.

Affiliation Windows as a Result of Increased Service Commitment Lengths

Using the same rationale that completing a service commitment closer to retirement affects retention, one could expect it to also affect the willingness of those who separate to affiliate to the RCs. Specifically, affiliation probability is highest for pilots who separate after initial ADSC completion, and decreases thereafter. Historical affiliation rates by CYOS, then, would underestimate the affiliation ceiling, because it would not account for the affiliation behavior of pilots held in the RegAF by a longer commitment. Thus, if the service commitment completion point is moved closer to retirement, the TFSC model requires affiliation rates to be adjusted accordingly.

We used GBMs to map the relationship between affiliation to the AFR and ANG and the same variables as before (YOSE, YORE, and flying community). We then used the same method as before to adjust affiliation rates for longer service commitment lengths by manipulating YOSE values.[3] Figure 3.4 shows an example of this adjustment for mobility pilots who enter the RegAF population in CYOS 2 under 10-year versus 13-year TFSC lengths (both using affiliation patterns as predicted by the GBM). The overall height of the shaded area in the sand chart reflects the percentage lost from the RegAF, while the blue-colored sections indicate the maximum percentage available to affiliate to the AFR and ANG. Affiliation rates are similar for pilots who separate near the TFSC completion point (CYOS 12 for the top panel, compared with CYOS 15 for the bottom panel). The main difference is that the adjustment allows for slightly higher affiliation rates in CYOS 16 through 20, since many pilots would not have had the opportunity to affiliate earlier under a longer service commitment. A comparison of the two panels also illustrates the reality that holding pilots in the RegAF longer will reduce the supply of affiliations available to the RCs, because the blue area is much smaller under the 13-year TFSC, even with the adjustment.

---

[3] One key difference between affiliation rates and loss rates is that affiliation rates are indexed only by CYOS, whereas loss rates are indexed by CYOS and entry CYOS. Expected loss rates hinge on entry CYOS because the latter determines separation eligibility, but affiliation rates only apply to pilots once they have already separated. Therefore, there was no strong reason to customize affiliation rates according to entry CYOS, and this simplification significantly reduced the number of constraints in the model and thus computation time to solve. The affiliation rates enter the model as a weighted average of predicted affiliation profiles for each entry CYOS.

Figure 3.4. Percentage of Mobility Pilots Lost from the Regular Air Force by Affiliation Status for Total Force Service Commitment Lengths of 10 Years (Top Panel) and 13 Years (Bottom Panel)

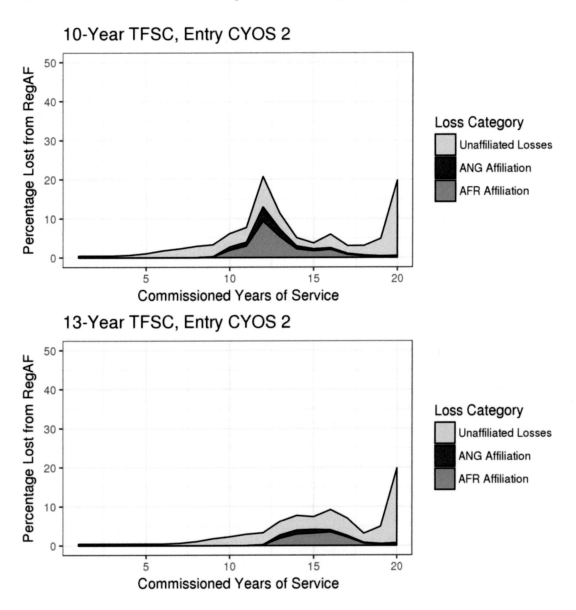

SOURCE: Authors' calculations from personnel data.

Adjusted Retention and Affiliation Patterns Form the Basis of Our Total Force Service Commitment Analysis

With plausible adjustments for retention and affiliation patterns under increased service commitment lengths, it is now possible to assess the potential impact of a TFSC policy on the long-term pilot inventory. The results in this chapter show that the model inputs for TFSC scenarios with longer service commitments will reflect better retention in all components, but also a reduction in the supply of pilots who leave the RegAF and affiliate to the RCs. However, the new possibility of transferring pilots from the RegAF to the RCs through a modified and expanded Palace Chase program (discussed in Chapter Two) could help to offset some of the reduced affiliations. The next chapter discusses the results of the inventory modeling in the context of the interplay between these forces.

Chapter 4. How Would a Total Force Service Commitment Policy Affect Pilot Shortages?

In this chapter, we use the TFSC model to examine the question of how a TFSC policy would affect pilot shortages by comparing projected inventories with Air Force pilot requirements.[1] We first examine the planned pilot production levels provided by the Air Force Directorate of Training and Readiness (AF/A3T). Then, knowing that the planned production results indicate that the pilot shortage will continue, we consider results where the model is permitted to reallocate some production across flying communities within prescribed, but slightly higher, limits that were also provided by AF/A3T.

A Total Force Service Commitment Policy Reduces, but Does Not Eliminate, Shortages Under Planned Production Levels

This section presents results under the Air Force's planned levels of pilot production.[2] In this version of the TFSC model, planned levels of production are used as input into the model for each component and pilot community, regardless of the manning situation, to show the result of Air Force production planning on the inventory (assuming the Air Force accurately executes the production targets).

---

[1] Requirements data were provided by AF/A3T and reflect the official planning assumptions at the time of the study. A3T projections are informed primarily by the Manpower Programming and Execution System (MPES). The requirements totals include pilot authorizations for staff and support positions.

[2] These planned production levels are the result of a lengthy process. *Production* in this modeling context means the successful graduation from UPT. The total production for each component is specified in the undergraduate planning program guidance letter (UPPGL), which is a continuously updated and more detailed version of the undergraduate program guidance letter (UPGL). The UPPGL needs to be continuously updated as the aircrew crisis worsens and the plans to rectify the situation change. The UPPGL is a document that allows the major commands (e.g., Air Education and Training Command) to get ahead of the budgetary process so that they can plan for increases in capacity to go along with the changes in the UPPGL. AF/A3TF uses the projected graduate program guidance letter (GPGL) along with the total component production specified in the UPPGL to distribute the total component production to the major weapon systems. There are two versions of the GPGL: one that specifies production in the most immediate year and a second version that specifies production two to three years out. The graduate program requirements document (GPRD) is the document that specifies graduate level requirements for four or more years out. The Programmed Flying Training (PFT) conference convenes annually and is a working group comprised of the major commands, the National Guard Bureau, Air Force Reserve Command, and AF/A3T to determine the number of flying hours available for training, from which the Air Force determines the number of instructor pilots and the number of new pilots that can be experienced in a given year for two to three years out, which informs creation of the second version of the GPGL.

The Majority of the Current and Future Pilot Shortage Resides in the Fighter Pilot Community

Before describing the outcomes of implementing a TFSC policy, it is first necessary to establish a baseline result for comparison purposes. To represent the status quo in which current policies continue unabated, we conducted a model run in which all losses reflect a 10-year service commitment and the Palace Chase path is closed. Figure 4.1 shows the annual shortages for the RegAF (top panel) and RCs (bottom panel) separately by flying community from FY17 through FY40. As indicated in Chapter One, near-term RegAF pilot shortages primarily reside in the fighter pilot community, but shortages also arise in the mobility pilot community starting in FY29. The RCs have enduring shortages in several pilot communities, but the majority of their unmet requirements are also in the fighter pilot community.

Figure 4.1. Annual Shortages for the Regular Air Force (Top Panel) and Reserve Components (Bottom Panel) in Baseline Scenario with 10-Year Service Commitments and No Palace Chase Transfers

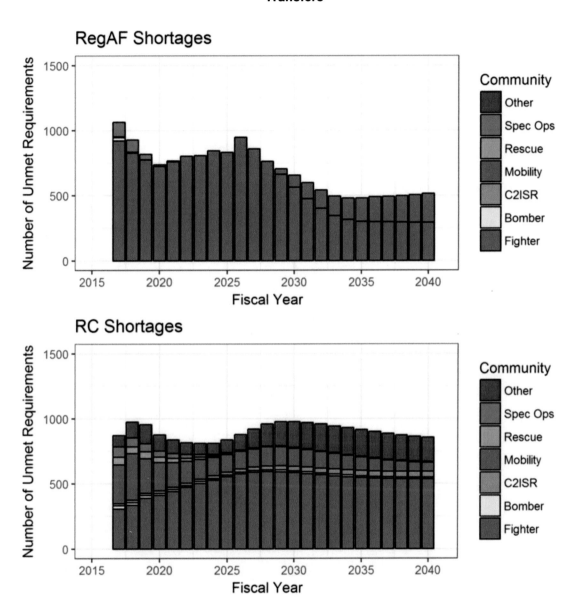

SOURCE: Authors' calculations from model results.
NOTES: "Other" community includes pilots in 11E, 11K, and 11G specialties. C2ISR (command, control, intelligence, surveillance, and reconnaissance) includes pilots in the 11R specialty.

Under Planned Production Levels, a Total Force Service Commitment Policy with Lengthier Service Commitments Is Unable to Close the Fighter Pilot Gap

Given that the most-acute pilot shortages are in the fighter pilot community, we begin by showing the impact of a TFSC policy on fighter pilot manning. Figure 4.2 compares the annual Total Force fighter pilot inventory with the number of Total Force fighter pilot requirements in the baseline scenario, as well as TFSC scenarios of 11-, 13-, and 15-year service commitment lengths. As expected, increasing the service commitment length improves the Total Force inventory in each case. However, all scenarios lead to a steady state that is well short of requirements. Even a dramatically increased service commitment of 15 years produces a limited reduction in the Total Force fighter pilot shortage, from 741 to 553 by FY40.

Figure 4.2. Total Force Fighter Pilot Requirements (Red Line) Versus Inventory (Blue Line)

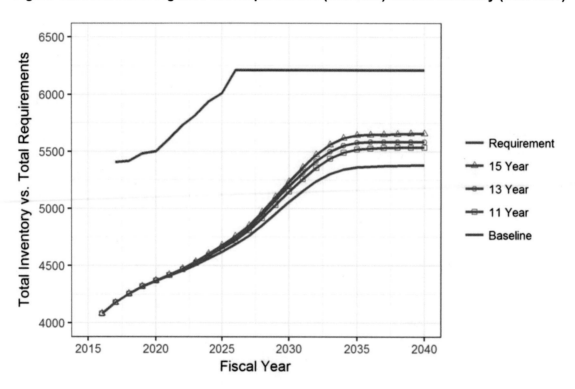

SOURCE: Authors' calculations from model results.
NOTE: Baseline scenario assumes a 10-year commitment and does not allow Palace Chase transfers.

The main reason for the limited influence of the TFSC policy on the shortage of fighter pilots is that the gains from improved retention are partly offset by a decrease in affiliations to the RCs (Figure 4.3). All TFSC scenarios result in significant steady-state improvements in RegAF health, but successively longer service commitments worsen RC fighter pilot shortages (especially in the AFR, which depends heavily on affiliations for obtaining new personnel). In theory, the Palace Chase path partly exists (in this version of a TFSC policy) to compensate the RCs for lost affiliations during the "bathtub" years.[3] Yet, while significant RC shortages exist,

---

[3] The "bathtub" years refer to the fact that increasing the RegAF service commitment by x years causes there to be zero separation-eligible RegAF pilots for x years while the new cohorts are under the longer service commitment. If zero RegAF pilots are eligible to separate because of the longer commitments, then the affiliations essentially go to zero. This happened in FY10–FY11 when the new cohorts who came in under the 10-year ADSC in FY99 continued to serve out their ADSCs in the RegAF, while those who came in FY98 and prior finished out their 8-year ADSCs.

the model opts to minimize Palace Chase transfers to avoid worsening the RegAF pilot shortage. This leads to a scenario in which either RC pilot health is sacrificed for the health of the RegAF or RegAF pilot health is sacrificed for the health of the RCs. Thus, planned production levels are insufficient to meet the needs of the Total Force, even if retention were substantially improved by longer service commitments.

Figure 4.3. Unmet Fighter Requirements by Component in FY40 for Different Total Force Service Commitment Scenarios

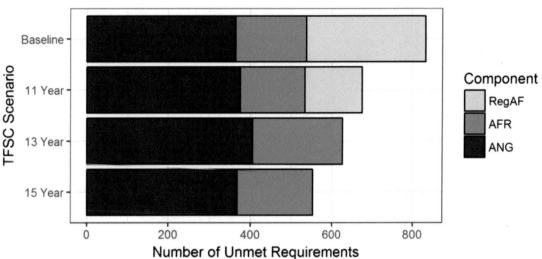

SOURCE: Authors' calculations from model results.
NOTE: Baseline scenario assumes a 10-year commitment and does not allow Palace Chase transfers.

A Combination of Retention Improvements and Palace Chase Flexibility Prevents Mobility Pilot Shortages

If no actions are taken, the baseline scenario shows a persistent RC mobility pilot shortage, as well as a RegAF mobility pilot shortage that emerges starting in FY29. Figure 4.4 summarizes how a TFSC policy might affect this potential outcome. In the baseline case, the decreasing RegAF mobility pilot inventory falls below requirements in FY29, while the RC mobility pilot inventory is short of the requirements for the entire period, FY16 through FY40 (which reflects the same shortage information presented in Figure 4.1). However, unlike the results for the fighter pilot community, the TFSC policy works as intended to mitigate or prevent shortages for mobility pilots. In the case of the 11-year TFSC, for example, the model takes advantage of better RegAF retention and holds onto enough mobility pilots to all but prevent the RegAF mobility pilot shortage. At the same time, it uses the Palace Chase path to apply surplus pilots

---

For two years, there were no new cohorts hitting separation eligibility, which caused a severe decrease in affiliations to the RC.

from other communities to the RC mobility pilot shortage. Further scenarios with higher TFSCs, such as the 13-year TFSC scenario in Figure 4.4, show a very similar picture. The main difference between the 11-year case and scenarios with longer TFSCs is that the model foresees better RegAF inventories in the future, and is therefore free to transfer surplus RegAF mobility pilots to the RCs starting in FY25 (which is why the RegAF inventory drops precipitously in that year).

Figure 4.4. Mobility Requirements (Red Line) Versus Inventory (Blue Line) for Regular Air Force (Top Panel) and Reserve Components (Bottom Panel)

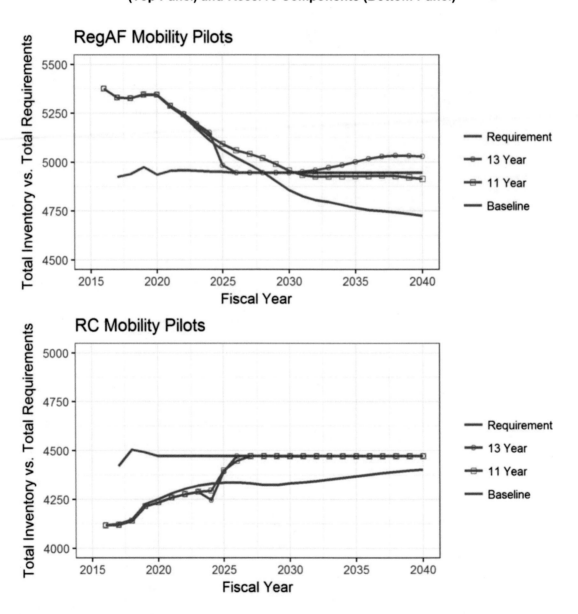

SOURCE: Authors' calculations from model results.
NOTE: Baseline scenario assumes a 10-year commitment and does not allow Palace Chase transfers. Results for 15-year TFSC are omitted for clarity, as they only differ in the size of the RegAF surplus in later years.

28

Overall, a Total Force Service Commitment Policy Reduces, but Does Not Eliminate, Total Force Pilot Shortages

Finally, Figure 4.5 summarizes the overall impact of the TFSC policy on the projected Total Force pilot shortages for a service commitment length of 11 years. Compared with the baseline case, the projections for a TFSC scenario with an 11-year commitment show close to a 50 percent reduction in unmet requirements by FY40. Furthermore, the combination of better retention (i.e., increased TARS and TRRS) and additional flexibility from the Palace Chase program addresses the needs of all communities except fighter pilots. Given that none of the TFSC scenarios that we examined was able to produce enough fighter pilots so that inventory levels matched fighter pilot requirements across the Total Force (see Figure 4.3), we now turn to scenarios that permit increases in production to understand better the future utility of a TFSC policy in addressing fighter pilot health.

Figure 4.5. Annual Total Force Pilot Shortages Under a Total Force Service Commitment of 11 Years Compared with Baseline Totals

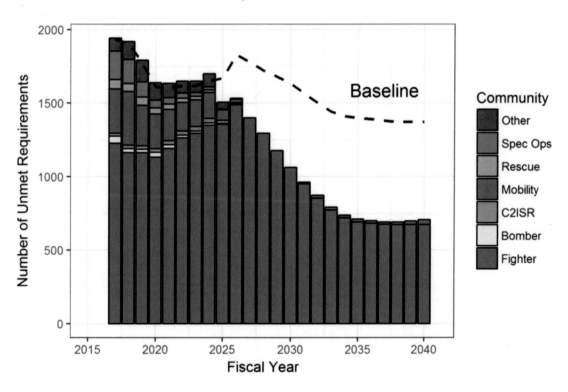

SOURCE: Authors' calculations from model results.
NOTES: "Other" community includes pilots in 11E, 11K, and 11G specialties. C2ISR includes pilots in the 11R specialty.

Reallocating Production Results Points to the Need for Increased Fighter Pilot Production

In the previous results, the production of new pilots follows the planned levels in perpetuity, regardless of the inventory in each pilot community. Given that policymakers understand that fighter pilot health requires higher levels of production in the near and medium terms, we created a variant of the TFSC model that has some flexibility in setting community-specific production levels, so long as different production levels help meet the model's goal of matching inventories to requirements. The following list enumerates the specific limitations that we place on production decisions in the model:

- Total Force production cannot exceed the planned total in each year through FY20, and is capped at 1,350 per year thereafter.
- Pilot-community-specific production cannot be less than 90 percent of the planned level.
- RegAF production cannot exceed theoretical limitations for each pilot community (provided by AF/A3TF) that steadily increase over time. For example, fighter pilot production builds from 284 in FY17 to 352 in FY24, and mobility pilot production builds from 269 to 490 in the same period.
- RC production cannot exceed planned levels.
- After the buildup through FY24, annual production in each community cannot deviate from the previous year by more than 3 percent to ensure stability over time.

These limitations guide the adjusted production levels according to career field management realities. The new parameters ensure that total production remains at or near planned levels, so that the solution does not call for a major reorganization of the training pipeline. Rather, these changes allow the model to reallocate production capacity across communities and components, potentially to bring the fighter and mobility pilot production levels in line with what is required for health and sustainability (hence, we refer to these results as being under *reallocated* production levels). The restrictions also enforce a production floor of 90 percent of the planned level and restrict deviations in the long term to 3 percent annually, to promote the consistency over time that characterizes the planning process. Finally, the restrictions do not permit any increase in RC production, because such increases were deemed unlikely through discussions with action officers and subject-matter experts in AF/A3TF.[4]

Reallocated Pilot Production Levels Are Close to Planned Levels, with a Shift Toward Fighter Pilot Production

First, Figure 4.6 compares the planned production levels that underlie the previous results with the reallocated production levels under a service commitment of 10 years. The clear result is that

---

[4] We settled on these limitations after examining many other, less restrictive boundaries for the Total Force limit and community/component-specific limits, as well as the year-to-year deviations.

the model moves production to the fighter and mobility pilot communities in anticipation of shortages, while reducing production in other areas where planned production is higher than needed for sustainment under the loss patterns we have assumed. This pattern is consistent across different TFSC lengths, except that the maximum reallocated fighter and mobility pilot production seen is less with longer commitments, as fewer new pilots are needed to replace losses.

Figure 4.6. Average Annual Regular Air Force Production Under Total Force Service Commitment of 10 Years: Planned Versus Reallocated Scenarios

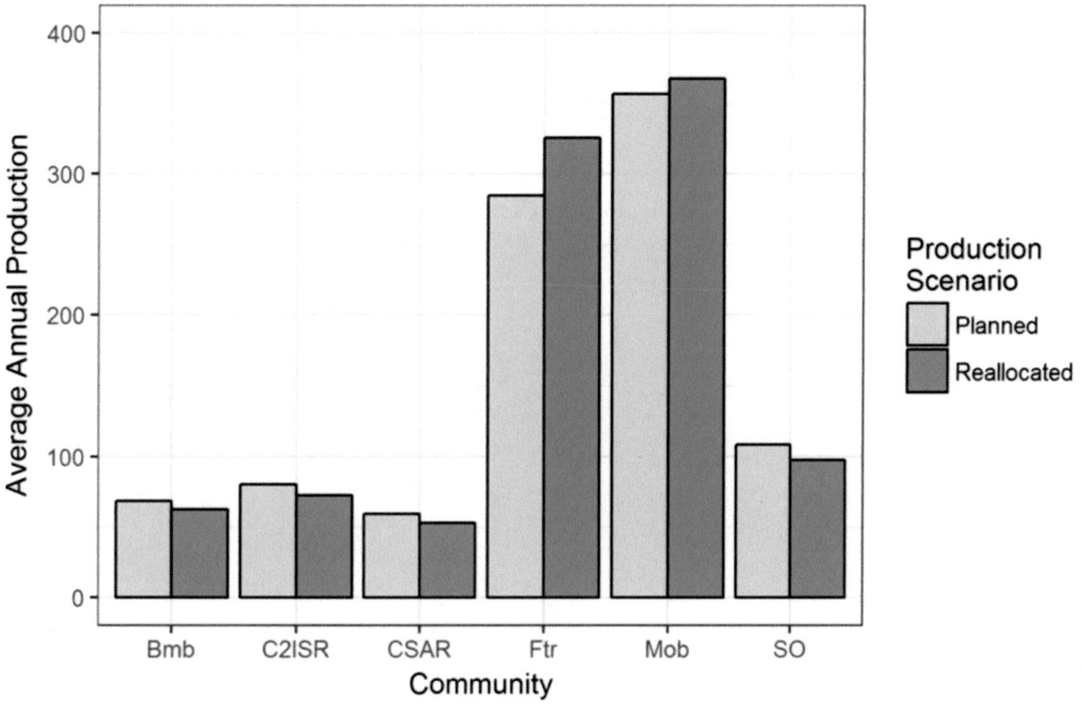

SOURCE: Authors' calculations from model results.
NOTE: The reallocated production scenario allows Palace Chase transfers, because the availability of Palace Chase affects production and allows more RC requirements to be met. Bmb = bomber; C2ISR = command and control, intelligence, surveillance, and reconnaissance; CSAR = combat search and rescue; Ftr = fighter; Mob = mobility; SO = special operations.

Additional Capacity to Produce Fighter Pilots Is Sufficient to End Shortages Without an Increase in Commitment Length

If pilot production changes such as those summarized in Figure 4.6 were feasible, they would change the dynamics of the TFSC policy in the fighter pilot community. Figure 4.7 illustrates the new dynamics by showing fighter pilot inventory projections for the baseline scenario (i.e., planned production) and several scenarios involving reallocated production levels. For the RegAF (shown in the top panel of the figure), the ability to reallocate production within the prescribed limits enables the model to bridge the gap between future inventory and requirements.

31

The only difference between the reallocated scenarios lies in the timeline associated with meeting all requirements. However, the increased production alone provides only a slight benefit to the RCs relative to the baseline, because affiliations alone do not provide enough fighter pilots to address RC shortages. Only the combination of increased RegAF fighter pilot production and additional Palace Chase transfers to the RCs can bring the Total Force fighter pilot inventory on par with the number of requirements.

Furthermore, the results under reallocated production indicate that longer commitments produce only minimal inventory improvements if increases in fighter pilot production are possible. The main reason for this result is that increases in service commitment length apply only to new cohorts, and, therefore, it takes at least 10 years before the new cohorts change the inventory relative to what it would have been under the current service commitment length. By the time these impacts begin to materialize in the RegAF, the fighter pilot production increases have already raised fighter pilot inventory levels close to the number of fighter pilot requirements. Rather than changing the inventory trajectory, a consistent result has been that increased service commitment lengths mostly affect the steady-state production level once the inventory has reached healthy levels.

Figure 4.7. Fighter Pilot Requirements (Red Line) Versus Inventory (Blue Line) for the Regular Air Force (Top Panel) and Reserve Components (Bottom Panel)

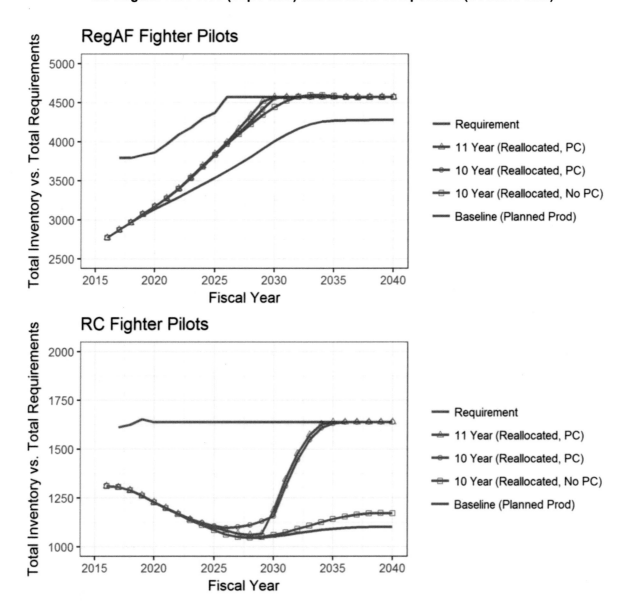

Reallocated Production with a 10-Year Commitment Meets All Requirements Before FY40

Figure 4.8 sums up the results under reallocated production by showing the pilot shortages for the RegAF and RCs with no increase in service commitment length, compared with the total pilot shortage number from the baseline scenario shown in Figure 4.1. In the RegAF, the pilot production changes eliminate all shortages by FY31. For the RCs, nonfighter shortages decline precipitously once the first cohorts of pilots become eligible for Palace Chase in FY25. RC fighter shortages do not begin to decline until after FY30, because more fighter pilots are available for Palace Chase once RegAF health is achieved.

Figure 4.8. Annual Shortages for the Regular Air Force (Top Panel) and RC (Bottom Panel) in Reallocated Production Scenario with 10-Year Commitments and Palace Chase Transfers

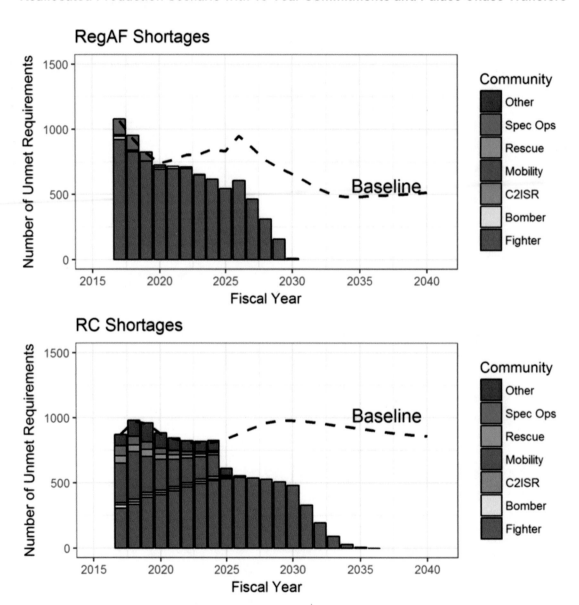

SOURCE: Authors' calculations from model results.
NOTES: "Other" community includes pilots in 11E, 11K, and 11G specialties. C2ISR includes pilots in the 11R specialty.

Summary

These results indicate that whether a TFSC policy could contribute to a solution to the aircrew crisis depends on multiple factors. The effectiveness of the TFSC policy depends on the community or component with the shortage as well as the expected flexibility in transfers and affiliations. Our model results show that a TFSC policy with longer service commitments can partially mitigate pilot shortages if production plans are unalterable, but that the benefits of longer service commitments become less important if certain pilot production adjustments are possible. The following chapter concludes with a discussion of the policy implications of these results.

Chapter 5. Conclusion on the Impact of a Total Force Service Commitment Policy with Lengthier Service Commitments

Continued shortages have opened the door to policy solutions aiming to (quickly) increase the pilot inventory at any point in the pilot career life cycle. The intuitive appeal of using a TFSC policy with increases in service commitment length to raise the expected number of years that new pilots serve in the Air Force prompted this exploratory Total Force policy analysis. In conducting this analysis, we arrived at the following general conclusions to guide decisionmaking in this area.

Whether a Total Force Service Commitment Policy Can Bring Inventories into Alignment Hinges on the Size of Retention Gains Relative to Shortages

Whether a TFSC policy brings pilot inventories in balance with requirements depends on whether the inventory gains of increased retention are large enough to cover the Total Force pilot shortfall. Regarding the most acute shortfall in the fighter pilot community, retention increases from longer service commitments were sufficient to meet RegAF demand in the steady state, but did not produce enough gains to bring the RCs into balance. Even if longer service commitments were to substantially improve long-run fighter pilot retention, the planned levels of production are insufficient to bring the Total Force inventories in line with the requirements structure.

Production Adjustments Are Necessary to Fully Address Long-Run Shortages

In all the cases examined, the only scenarios capable of fully addressing the shortages in all communities included adjustments to production plans. However, reaching the desired inventory levels does not require growth in the overall number of pilots produced, but rather a reallocation of existing production capacity toward communities in need. If policymakers desire to maintain the current requirements structure, the most pressing need is for growth in fighter pilot production (and absorption), along with sufficient flow to the AFR and ANG to address RC shortfalls.

The Timing and Size of Total Force Service Commitment Impacts Make the Policy Unlikely to Play a Major Role in Addressing the Aircrew Crisis

Building on the previous point, if the production adjustments described in the previous chapter are feasible, this means that a TFSC policy would have limited effectiveness in addressing the most-acute shortages of the aircrew crisis. The limited effectiveness of the TFSC policy stems from the relatively modest projected improvements in the fighter pilot inventory and the delay in the effect of a policy change involving service commitment lengths. The analysis shows that Total Force pilot production adjustments are necessary to decrease the fighter pilot shortages, and such adjustments would have a much more immediate impact on the problem at hand.

Persistent Shortages Create a Trade-Off Between Regular Air Force and Reserve Component Health

A consistent pattern throughout these analyses is that longer service commitments will worsen RC health unless Palace Chase transfers replace the pilots who would have separated and affiliated in the absence of the change. However, the TFSC model as programmed, to be consistent with guidance from Air Force planners, was consistently reluctant to use the Palace Chase program to send fighter pilots to the RCs because of the RegAF shortages that would accrue. This dynamic produced outcomes in which RC health worsened under longer service commitments because the RCs did not receive enough Palace Chase transfers to make up for lost affiliations. While the TFSC policy was initially expected to benefit the RCs, these results showed that improvements in RegAF health often came at the expense of the RCs.

Affiliation Flexibility Significantly Affects Reserve Component Shortfalls

A key difference between the RC mobility and fighter pilot communities is that there is historical precedent for multiple RegAF pilot communities to affiliate and become RC mobility pilots, whereas RC fighter pilots are almost exclusively former RegAF fighter pilots. This additional flexibility inherent in mobility pilot affiliations allowed the RegAF to capitalize on improved retention, while using the Palace Chase path to send pilots from other communities (such as special operations and C2ISR) to fill RC mobility pilot requirements. This finding suggests that additional paths to filling RC fighter pilot requirements (such as increased cross-training) could be one tool to deal with the trade-off between RegAF and RC health under longer service commitments.

Other Potential Limitations of a Total Force Service Commitment Policy Could Partly Offset Inventory Improvements

It is necessary in a steady-state analysis to assume that certain workforce parameters, such as available production levels, will continue into the future. However, there are second- and third-order consequences of implementing a TFSC policy that this analysis does not account for. For example, a key concern is whether longer service commitments will create recruiting challenges, reducing the attractiveness of the pilot career fields and impacting future production. Longer service commitments could also change the composition of incoming pilot candidates in a way that alters training attrition and pilot retention over a career. Before implementing a TFSC policy, further research should examine these and other potential consequences.

Summary

The prospect of sustained retention difficulties (driven by a strong market for ex-military pilots in the civilian sector) has naturally led policymakers to consider adjusting service commitments as a potential remedy. This study confirmed that a policy of lengthier commitments and increased flexibility in cross-flow to the RCs could produce a Total Force that meets more requirements, but it could not eliminate shortages in every pilot community across the Total Force without further changes to production. Furthermore, our work provides little analytical reason to pursue a Total Force service commitment policy with longer commitments, given that there are other potential challenges that this analysis cannot address. These results paint a clear picture that increasing production (and absorption) is a required way forward in addressing this aircrew crisis.

Appendix A. Technical Model Formulation

The primary tool used in this project is a linear programming model embedded in SAS programming language. We refer to it as the "TFSC model."

TFSC Model

RAND has developed a family of inventory models, implemented as SAS-based linear programming models, with very similar characteristics. The first of these was the Total Force Blue Line (TFBL) model discussed in the main body of this document. TFBL was built to project Total Force rated officer inventories. Line graphs depicting projected manpower requirements and inventories conventionally use a red line (RL) for the requirements and a blue line (BL) for the inventories; consequently, this model became known as the Air Force RL/BL model. A variation of the model was later adapted for more-detailed analysis of the Air Force's remotely piloted aircraft (RPA) officer force, for the Air Force's career enlisted aviators, and also for testing out some "Force of the Future" policies across the Air Force in general. For the project underlying this report, we modified the TFBL model to address the impact of lengthier service commitments served across the Total Force on future inventory levels, which added some additional complexity.

A linear programming model can be specified using the following constructs:

- *Scalars* are single values defined for recurring use in various expressions. For example, the scalar *fyfirst* is defined to have a value of 2016, which is the first FY represented in the model.
- The demographic subgroups represented in the model are referred to as its *dimensions*.
- *Parameters* are fixed values provided as inputs to the model. Inputs to the TFSC model include arrays of rated officer requirements, retention rates, the beginning inventory, and other empirical or policy-related values.
- *Variables* are values that change as the model's solving algorithm seeks an optimal solution.
- *Indices* identify the various arrays of values—parameters and variables—used in the model. For example, arrays of requirements used as inputs to the model are indexed by component, community, and FY dimensions. In the expressions used in this appendix to define the model, indices appear as subscripts.
- An *index set* specifies the members of a dimensional index or a combination of indices. For example, the index set representing CYOS contains the members 0 to 30.
- By systematically changing the values of the variables, the model minimizes or maximizes an *objective function*, a value equal to a sum of selected variables.
- *Boundary conditions* fix the values of certain subsets of variables. For example, inventories in the first FY represented in the model are fixed to equal the initial inventories entered as parameters in the model.

39

- The model adheres to *constraints*—equations expressed using parameters and variables.

For consistency, sets are denoted by an "s_", parameters are denoted by a "p_", and variables are denoted by a "v_".

Data Dimensions

The model includes eight dimensions of that define the rated officer requirements, and inventories: component, rated category, major weapon system (MWS), population, CYOS, entry year, and FY. These dimensions are defined as follows:

- **Component.** The model includes all three components in the Total Force Air Force. The subscript c identifies this dimension.
- **Rated category.** This model includes two rated officer categories: pilots and RPA pilots. The subscript r identifies this dimension.
- **MWS.** The model considers nine officer career fields that span all three components and the two rated categories. In the expressions below, the subscript s identifies this dimension.
- **Population.** The model considers three populations to determine eligibility to transfer within the Palace Chase construct. In the expressions below, the subscript p identifies this dimension.
- **CYOS.** The model includes up to 30 commissioned years of service. This model employs CYOS = 0 for inventory with less than one complete year of service. CYOS = 1 indicates inventory with service greater than or equal to one but less than two complete years. The subscript y identifies this dimension.
- **Entry year.** The model includes the entry year when a pilot successfully graduates from UPT to determine separation eligibility separate from CYOS. The subscript e identifies this dimension.
- **Fiscal year.** The model can be extended for any number of fiscal years into the future. For this project, the starting inventory was taken as the end of FY16 and projections are made through FY60. The subscript f identifies this dimension.

Technical Model Formulation

What follows is a detailed description of the TFSC model. We specify the index sets and indices, scalars, parameters, and variables that comprise the objective function and constraints of the TFSC model and then provide the objective function and constraints.

Sets and Indices

We will use the following sets in the model:

- s_fy, set of fiscal years (FY) , f ∈ s_fy = {fyfirst, ..., fylast}

- s_cy, set of commissioned years of services (CYOS), y ∈ s_cy = {cyfirst, ..., cylast}

- s_ey, set of entry CYOS, e ∈ s_ey = {eyfirst, ..., eylast}

- s_rcat, set of rated categories, r ∈ s_rcat = {Plt, RPA}

- s_compo, set of components, c ∈ s_compo = {RegAF, AFR, ANG}

- s_icat, set of inventory categories, s ∈ s_icat = {Bmb, C2ISR, CSAR, Ftr, Mob, SO, RPA11, RPA12, RPA18, 11B, 11E, 11F, 11G, 11H, 11K, 11M, 11R, 11S, 11U, 12U, 18X}

- s_bcat, set of requirement categories, s ∈ s_bcat = = {rBmb, rC2ISR, rCSAR, rFtr, rMob, rSO, rRPA, r11B, r11E, r11F, r11G, r11H, r11K, r11M, r11R, r11S, r11U, r12U, r18X}

- s_pop, set of population segments, p ∈ s_pop = {Legacy, PreWin, Window, ADSC}

- s_cy_ey, possible current CYOS and entry CYOS combinations, ⊆ s_cy × s_ey

- s_ivld, set of valid inventory category combinations, ⊆ s_rcat × s_compo × s_icat × s_pop

- s_bvld, set of valid requirement category combinations, ⊆ s_rcat × s_compo × s_bcat

- s_rqmt, requirement categories by FY, ⊆ s_rcat × s_compo × s_bcat × s_fy

- s_asgn, set of valid assignments, ⊆ s_rcat × s_compo × s_icat × s_pop × s_rcat × s_compo × s_bcat

- s_avld, set of valid assignments by FY, ⊆ s_rcat × s_compo × s_icat × s_pop × s_rcat × s_compo × s_bcat × s_fy

- s_allow_afil, set of possible affiliation paths, ⊆ s_rcat × s_compo × s_icat × s_pop × s_rcat × s_compo × s_icat × s_pop

- s_trans_afil, possible affiliations paths by CYOS, entry CYOS, and FY, ⊆ s_rcat × s_compo × s_icat × s_pop × s_rcat × s_compo × s_icat × s_pop × s_cy × s_ey × s_fy

- s_bal_afil, set of aggregated affiliation paths by FY, ⊆ s_rcat × s_compo × s_icat × s_rcat × s_compo × s_icat × s_fy

- s_afil_orig, set of possible affiliation origin points, ⊆ s_rcat × s_compo × s_icat × s_pop

- s_afil_orig_fy, set of possible affiliation origin points by FY, ⊆ s_rcat × s_compo × s_icat × s_pop × s_fy

- s_init, set of initial inventories for all inventory categories, ⊆ s_rcat × s_compo × s_icat × s_pop × s_cy × s_ey

- s_aginv_ey, set of inventory categories aggregated over CYOS, $\subseteq$ s_rcat $\times$ s_compo $\times$ s_icat $\times$ s_pop $\times$ s_ey $\times$ s_fy

- s_aginv, set of inventory categories aggregated over CYOS and entry CYOS, $\subseteq$ s_rcat $\times$ s_compo $\times$ s_icat $\times$ s_pop $\times$ s_fy

- s_inv, set of maximally dis-aggregated inventory indices, $\subseteq$ s_rcat $\times$ s_compo $\times$ s_icat $\times$ s_pop $\times$ s_cy $\times$ s_ey $\times$ s_fy

- s_ent, set of production plans or limits, $\subseteq$ s_rcat $\times$ s_compo $\times$ s_icat $\times$ s_pop $\times$ s_fy

- s_ent_lb, set of minimum production values, $\subseteq$ s_rcat $\times$ s_compo $\times$ s_icat $\times$ s_pop $\times$ s_fy

- s_dst_ent, distribution of CYOS for newly-produced pilots to enter into, $\subseteq$ s_rcat $\times$ s_compo $\times$ s_icat $\times$ s_pop $\times$ s_cy $\times$ s_ey

- s_total_prod, set of total annual production limits for each rated category, $\subseteq$ s_rcat $\times$ s_fy

- s_ireg, set of RegAF inventory categories for a single population, $\subseteq$ s_rcat $\times$ s_icat $\times$ s_cy $\times$ s_fy $\times$ s_ivld

- s_ireg_ripi, set of permissible rated category-population combinations, $\subseteq$ s_rcat $\times$ s_pop

- s_palace_min, set of aggregated inventory categories to use in imposing minimum palace chase requirements, $\subseteq$ s_icat $\times$ s_fy

- s_good_ar, set of affiliation rates, $\subseteq$ s_rcat $\times$ s_compo $\times$ s_icat $\times$ s_pop $\times$ s_cy

- s_force_trans, set of planned transfers, $\subseteq$ s_rcat $\times$ s_compo $\times$ s_icat $\times$ s_pop $\times$ s_rcat $\times$ s_compo $\times$ s_icat $\times$ s_pop $\times$ s_cy $\times$ s_fy

- s_force_trans_pop, set of planned transfers by population, $\subseteq$ s_rcat $\times$ s_compo $\times$ s_icat $\times$ s_pop $\times$ s_rcat $\times$ s_compo $\times$ s_icat $\times$ s_pop $\times$ s_cy $\times$ s_ey $\times$ s_fy

- s_surv, set of survival rates, $\subseteq$ s_rcat $\times$ s_compo $\times$ s_icat $\times$ s_pop $\times$ s_cy $\times$ s_ey $\times$ s_fy

- s_pflow, set of population transitions, $\subseteq$ s_rcat $\times$ s_compo $\times$ s_pop $\times$ s_pop

- s_afil_flow, set of population transitions that take place only when pilots affiliate to the AFR or ANG, $\subseteq$ s_rcat $\times$ s_pop $\times$ s_pop

- s_pop_shift, set of transition points when pilots move to a new population, $\subseteq$ s_pop $\times$ s_cy $\times$ s_ey

Scalars

- cyfirst $= 0$

- cylast $= 30$

- fyfirst $= 2016$

- fylast $= 2075$

- eyfirst $= 1$

- eylast $= 6$

- prod_percent_delta $= 0.03$.

Parameters

We will use the following parameters in the model:

- p_bvld$_{rcs_b}$ specifies the valid requirement categories allowed in the model for rated category $r \in$ s_rcat, component $c \in$ s_compo, and requirement category $s_b \in$ s_bcat

- p_rqmt$_{rcs_bf}$ specifies the requirement for rated category $r \in$ s_rcat, component $c \in$ s_compo, requirement category $s_b \in$ s_bcat and FY $f \in$ s_fy

- p_allow_afil$_{r_1 c_1 s_1 p_1 r_2 c_2 s_2 p_2}$ the allowed affiliation paths from one rated category $r_1 \in$ s_rcat, component $c_1 \in$ s_compo, inventory category $s_1 \in$ s_icat, and population segment $p_1 \in$ s_pop to another rated category $r_2 \in$ s_rcat, component $c_2 \in$ s_compo, inventory category $s_2 \in$ s_icat, and population segment $p_2 \in$ s_pop

- p_init_inv$_{rcs_i pye}$ the starting inventory used to initialize the model for rated category $r \in$ s_rcat, component $c \in$ s_compo, inventory category $s_i \in$ s_icat, population segment $p \in$ s_pop, CYOS $y \in$ s_cy, and entry CYOS $e \in$ s_ey

- p_prod$_{rcs_i pf}$ the planned production levels (or upper bound for optimized model runs) for rated category $r \in$ s_rcat, component $c \in$ s_compo, inventory category $s_i \in$ s_icat, population segment $p \in$ s_pop, and FY $f \in$ s_fy

- p_prod_lb$_{rcs_i pf}$ is the lower bound on production for optimized production model runs for rated category $r \in$ s_rcat, component $c \in$ s_compo, inventory category $s_i \in$ s_icat, population segment $p \in$ s_pop, and FY $f \in$ s_fy

- p_dst_ent$_{rcspye}$ the CYOS distribution of when pilots graduate from UPT for rated category $r \in$ s_rcat, component $c \in$ s_compo, inventory category $s \in$ s_icat, population segment $p \in$ s_pop, CYOS $y \in$ s_cy, and entry CYOS $e \in$ s_ey

- p_total_prod$_{rf}$ is the Total Force production capacity for rated category $r \in$ s_rcat and FY $f \in$ s_fy

- p_afr_rate$_{rcspy}$ is the AFR historical affiliation rates for rated category $r \in$ s_rcat, component $c \in$ s_compo, inventory category $s \in$ s_icat, population segment $p \in$ s_pop, and FY $f \in$ s_fy

- p_ang_rate$_{rcspy}$ is the ANG historical affiliation rates for rated category $r \in$ s_rcat, component $c \in$ s_compo, inventory category $s \in$ s_icat, population segment $p \in$ s_pop, and FY $f \in$ s_fy

- p_force_trans$_{r_1 c_1 s_1 r_2 c_2 s_2 y f}$ contains the transfers from one rated category $r_1 \in$ s_rcat, component $c_1 \in$ s_compo, and inventory category $s_1 \in$ s_icat to another rated category $r_2 \in$ s_rcat, component $c_2 \in$ s_compo, and inventory category $s_2 \in$ s_icat for each CYOS $y \in$ s_cy and FY $f \in$ s_fy

- p_surv$_{rcspyef}$ is the survival rate (1-loss rate) for rated category $r \in$ s_rcat, component $c \in$ s_compo, inventory category $s \in$ s_icat, population segment $p \in$ s_pop, CYOS $y \in$ s_cy, and entry CYOS $e \in$ s_ey, entry FY $f \in$ s_fy

- p_shift$_{pye}$ is the indicator when a person needs to move to the next population segment as they age by CYOS for $p \in$ s_pop, CYOS $y \in$ s_cy, and entry CYOS $e \in$ s_ey.

Variables

We will use the following variables in the model:

- v_unfill$_{rcsf} \geq 0$ is the number of unfilled requirements (meaning that there is not an officer available to be assigned to the requirement) for each rated category r, component c, requirement category s, and FY f for $(r, c, s, f) \in$ s_rqmt.

- v_asgn$_{r_i c_i s_i p_i r_r, c_r, s_r, f} \geq 0$ is the number of officers assigned from an inventory rated category r_i, component c_i, inventory category s_i and population segment p_i to a requirement rated category r_r, component c_r and requirement category s_r for each FY f for $(r_i, c_i, s_i, p_i, r_r, c_r, s_r, f) \in$ s_avld.

- v_inv$_{rcspyef} \geq 0$ is the number of personnel in the inventory at the end of each FY for each rated category r, component c, inventory category s, population segment p, CYOS y, entry CYOS e, and FY f for $(r, c, s, p, y, e, f) \in$ s_inv.

- v_unasgn$_{rcspf} \geq 0$ is the number of officers unassigned for each rated category r, component c, inventory category s, population segment p, and FY f for $(r, c, s, p, f) \in$ s_aginv.

- v_ent$_{rcspf} \geq 0$ is the number of entries for each rated category r, component c, inventory category s, population segment p, and FY f for $(r, c, s, p, f) \in$ s_ent.

- v_sep$_{rcspyef} \geq 0$ is the number of personnel who separate or retire for each rated category r, component c, inventory category s, population segment p, CYOS y, entry CYOS e, and FY f for $(r, c, s, p, y, e, f) \in$ s_inv.

- v_afil$_{r_1 c_1 s_1 p_1 r_2 c_2 s_2 p_2 y e f} \geq 0$ is the number of pilots who affiliate from one rated category r_1, component c_1, inventory category s_1, and population segment p_1 to another rated category r_2, component c_2, inventory category s_2, and population segment p_2 for each CY c, entry CY e and FY f for $(r_1, c_1, s_1, p_1, r_2, c_2, s_2, p_2, y, e, f) \in$ s_trans_afil

44

- v_aforig$_{rcspf}$ ≥ 0 is the number of pilots who would affiliate to the RC under historical affiliation patterns for each rated category r, component c, inventory category s, population segment p, and FY f for $(r, c, s, p, f) \in$ s_afil_orig_fy

- v_afpos$_{r_1c_1s_1r_2s_2c_2f}$ ≥ 0 is the number of positive deviations when calculated using the historical affiliation rate for each to and from inventory category from one rated category r_1, component c_1, and inventory category s_1 to another rated category r_2, component c_2, and inventory category s_2 for each FY f for $(r_1, c_1, s_1, r_2, s_2, c_2, f) \in$ s_bal_afil

- v_afneg$_{r_1c_1s_1r_2s_2c_2f}$ ≥ 0 is the number of negative deviations when calculated using the historical affiliation rate for each to and from inventory category from one rated category r_1, component c_1, and inventory category s_1 to another rated category r_2, component c_2, and inventory category s_2 for each FY f for $(r_1, c_1, s_1, r_2, s_2, c_2, f) \in$ s_bal_afil

- v_forcetrans$_{r_1c_1s_1p_1r_2s_2c_2p_2fey}$ ≥ 0 contains the transfers from one rated category $r_1 \in$ s_rcat, component $c_1 \in$ s_compo, and inventory category $s_1 \in$ s_icat to another rated category $r_2 \in$ s_rcat, component $c_2 \in$ s_compo, and inventory category $s_2 \in$ s_icat for each CYOS $y \in$ s_cy and FY $f \in$ s_fy for $(r_1, c_1, s_1, r_2, s_2, c_2, f, y) \in$ s_force_trans_pop

- v_palace$_{r_1c_1s_1p_1r_2c_2s_2p_2yef}$ ≥ 0 is the number of pilots that Palace Chase to the RC from one rated category r_1, component c_1, inventory category s_1, and population segment p_1 to another rated category r_2, component c_2, inventory category s_2, and population segment p_2 for each CY c, entry CY e and FY f for $(r_1, c_1, s_1, p_1, r_2, c_2, s_2, p_2, y, e, f) \in$ s_trans_afil

- v_popshift$_{rcspyef}$ ≥ 0 is the number of pilots that are transitioning into a new population for each rated category r, component c, inventory category s, population segment p, CYOS y, entry CYOS e, and FY f for $(r, c, s, p, y, e, f) \in$ s_inv.

Objective Function

In this model, we include six goals in the objective function, which can be thought of as multi-goal programming. The goals include minimizing unfilled requirements (jobs that cannot be filled by a rated officer), minimizing excess inventory (the number of rated officers who do not have a job), and minimizing the production of rated officers. Separately, we incentivize affiliations and palace chase transfers to happen much like they have historically happened by MWS. Since the objective function reflects multiple goals, it is necessary to determine the relative importance of each goal in order to produce meaningful results. After some experimentation, we chose to weight the first five goals equally while also adding a penalty of 5 to the use of Palace Chase (which incentivizes the model to prefer traditional affiliations over palace chase wherever possible).

$$\min \sum_{(r,c,s,p,f)\in s\_aginv \ni f>fyfirst} \text{v\_unasgn}_{rcspf}$$

$$+ \sum_{(r,c,b,f)\in s\_rqmt \ni f>fyfirst} (\text{p\_bvld}_{rcb} * \text{v\_unfill}_{rcbf})$$

$$+ \sum_{(r,c,s,p,f)\in s\_ent \ni f>fyfirst} \text{v\_ent}_{rcspf}$$

$$+ \sum_{(r_1,c_1,s_1,r_2,c_2,s_2,f)\in s\_bal\_afil \ni f>fyfirst} \text{v\_afpos}_{r_1 c_1 s_1 r_2 c_2 s_2 f}$$

$$+ \sum_{(r_1,c_1,s_1,r_2,c_2,s_2,f)\in s\_bal\_afil \ni f>fyfirst} \text{v\_afneg}_{r_1 c_1 s_1 r_2 c_2 s_2 f}$$

$$+ 5 * \left(\sum_{(r_1,c_1,s_1,p_1,r_2,c_2,s_2,p_2,y,e,f)\in s\_trans\_afil} \text{v\_palace}_{r_1 c_1 s_1 p_1 r_2 c_2 s_2 p_2 yef} \right)$$

Constraints

1. Unfilled requirements plus filled requirements (which are equal to assigned personnel) equal total requirements:

$$\sum_{(r_i,c_i,s_i,p_i)\in s\_ivld \ni (r_i,c_i,s_i,p_i,r_r,c_r,s_r,f)\in s\_avld} \text{v\_asgn}_{r_i c_i s_i p_i r_r c_r s_r f} + \text{v\_unfill}_{r_r c_r s_r f} = \text{p\_rqmt}_{r_r c_r s_r f}$$

$$\forall (r_r, c_r, s_r, f) \in \text{s\_rqmt}$$

2. Assigned personnel (which is equal to filled requirements) plus unassigned personnel equal total inventory:

$$\sum_{(r_r,c_r,s_r)\in s\_bvld \ni (r_i,c_i,s_i,p_i,r_r,c_r,s_r,f)\in s\_avld} \text{v\_asgn}_{r_i c_i s_i p_i r_r c_r s_r f} + \text{v\_unasgn}_{r_i,c_i,s_i,p_i,f}$$

$$= \sum_{(y,e)\in s\_cy\_ey \ni (r_i,c_i,s_i,p_i,y,e,f)\in s\_inv} \text{v\_inv}_{r_i c_i s_i p_i yef}$$

$$\forall (r_i, c_i, s_i, p_i, f) \in \text{s\_aginv}.$$

3. Nonpilot accessions are less than user-specified parameters:

$$\text{v\_ent}_{rcspf} \leq \text{p\_prod}_{rcspf}$$

$$\forall (r,c,s,p,f) \in \text{s\_ent} \ni f > \text{fyfirst}$$
$$\wedge ((c = RegAF \wedge r = Plt \wedge p = Prewin) \vee (c \neq RegAF \vee r = RPA \wedge p = ADSC)).$$

NOTE: To reduce the complexity of the problem, we often limit constraints to particular rated category/component/population combinations that they apply to. For example, since all new RegAF pilot production enters the "PreWin" population and all other new production enters the "ADSC" population, this and other production-related constraints only apply to RegAF & Plt & PreWin or non-RegAF/RPA & ADSC.

4. Nonpilot accessions are greater than user-specified parameters:

$$\text{v\_ent}_{rcspf} \geq \text{p\_prod\_lb}_{rcspf}$$

$$\forall (r,c,s,p,f) \in \text{s\_ent} \ni f > \text{fyfirst}$$
$$\wedge (c = RegAF \wedge ((r = Plt \wedge p = Prewin) \vee (r = RPA \wedge p = ADSC)).$$

5. Smoothflow production for consistency in production from year to year.
   NOTE: prod_percent_delta is a parameter that the user can specify to modulate the year-to-year changes in production. It sets a maximum limit on the percentage change in the previous year, ensuring some amount of production stability over time.

$$\text{v\_ent}_{rcspf-1} - \text{v\_ent}_{rcspf} \leq (prod\_percent\_delta * \text{v\_ent}_{rcspf-1}) + 1$$

$$\forall (r,c,s,p,f) \in \text{s\_ent} \ni f > \text{fyfirst+8}$$
$$\wedge ((c = RegAF \wedge r = Plt \wedge p = Prewin) \vee ((c \neq RegAF \vee c = RPA) \wedge p = ADSC)).$$

6. Smoothflow production for consistency in production from year to year (allow unlimited growth within other production constraints until 2025)

$$\text{v\_ent}_{rcspf-1} - \text{v\_ent}_{rcspf} \geq (-prod\_percent\_delta * \text{v\_ent}_{rcspf-1}) - 1$$

$$\forall (r,c,s,p,f) \in \text{s\_ent} \ni f > \text{fyfirst+8}$$
$$\wedge ((c = RegAF \wedge r = Plt \wedge p = Prewin) \vee ((c \neq RegAF \vee c = RPA) \wedge p = ADSC)).$$

7. Total Production cap for each rated category and FY for cases where production is optimized.

$$\sum_{\substack{c \in \text{s\_comp} \\ s \in \text{s\_icat} \\ p \in \text{s\_pop} \\ \ni (r,c,s,p,y) \in \text{s\_end} \\ \wedge((c=\text{RegAF} \wedge r=\text{Plt} \wedge p=\text{Prewin}) \vee \\ (c \neq \text{RegAF} \vee r=\text{RPA}) \wedge p=\text{Prewin}))}} \text{v\_ent}_{rcspf} \leq \text{p\_total\_prod}_{rf}$$

$$\forall (r, f) \in \text{s\_total\_prod} \ni f > \text{fyfirst}$$

8. Calculation of the number of pilots separating each year by applying annual loss rates.

$$\text{v\_sep}_{rcspyef} = \text{v\_inv}_{rcspy-1ef-1} * \left(1 - \text{p\_surv}_{rcspcyf}\right)$$

$$\forall (r, c, s, p, y, e, f) \in \text{s\_inv} \ni y \geq \text{cyfirst} \wedge y \geq e \wedge f > \text{fyfirst}$$
$$\wedge \neg (p = \text{Legacy} \wedge (f \geq \text{fyfirst} + 31 \vee e > \text{eyfirst} \vee cy < f - \text{fyfirst})$$
$$\wedge \neg (p = \text{Legacy} \wedge (y \geq \text{eylast} + f - \text{fyfirst}))$$

9. Legacy affiliations to ANG are less than specified fraction of separations

$$\sum_{\substack{r_2 \in \text{s\_rcat} \\ s_2 \in \text{s\_icat} \\ \ni (r_1,\text{RegAF},s_1,\text{Legacy},r_2,\text{ANG},s_2,\text{Legacy}) \in \text{s\_allow\_afil}}} \text{v\_afil}_{r_1\text{'RegAF'}s_1\text{'Legacy'}r_2\text{'ANG'}s_2\text{'Legacy'}y\text{'eyfirst'}f}$$

$$\leq \text{p\_angrate}_{r_1\text{'RegAF'}s_1\text{'Legacy'}y} * \text{v\_sep}_{r_1\text{'RegAF'}s_1\text{'Legacy'}y\text{'eyfirst'}f}$$

$$\forall (r_1, s_1, y, f) \in \text{s\_ireg} \ni cy > \text{cyfirst} \wedge (\text{fyfirst} < fy < \text{fyfirst} + 31) \wedge (cy \geq fy - \text{fyfirst})$$

10. Non-legacy affiliations to ANG are less than specified fraction of separations (all non-legacy affiliations go into the ARC ADSC population)

$$\sum_{\substack{r_2 \in \text{s\_rcat} \\ s_2 \in \text{s\_icat} \\ p \in \text{s\_pop} \\ e \in \text{s\_ey} \\ \ni (r_1,\text{RegAF},s_1,p,r_2,\text{ANG},s_2,\text{ADSC}) \in \text{s\_allow\_afil} \\ \wedge p \neq \text{'Legacy'}}} \text{v\_afil}_{r_1\text{'RegAF'}s_1 pr_2\text{'ANG'}s_2\text{'ADSC'}yef}$$

$$\leq \text{p\_angrate}_{r_1\text{'RegAF'}s_1\text{'ADSC'}y}$$

$$* \sum_{\substack{p \in \text{s\_pop} \\ e \in \text{s\_ey} \\ \ni (r_1,\text{RegAF},s_1,pyef) \in \text{s\_inv} \\ \wedge y \geq e \wedge p \neq \text{'Legacy'}}} \text{v\_sep}_{r_1\text{'RegAF'}s_1 pyef}$$

$$\forall (r_1, s_1, y, f) \in \text{s\_ireg} \ni cy > \text{cyfirst} \wedge (\text{fyfirst} < fy < \text{fyfirst} + 31) \wedge (cy \geq fy - \text{fyfirst})$$

11. Legacy affiliations to AFR are less than specified fraction of separations

$$\sum_{\substack{r_2 \in \text{s\_rcat} \\ s_2 \in \text{s\_icat} \\ \ni (r_1, \text{RegAF}, s_1, \text{Legacy}, r_2, \text{AFR}, s_2, \text{Legacy}) \in \text{s\_allow\_afil}}} \text{v\_afil}_{r_1\text{'RegAF'}s_1\text{'Legacy'}r_2\text{'AFR'}s_2\text{'Legacy'}y\text{'eyfirst'}f}$$

$$\leq \text{p\_angrate}_{r_1\text{'RegAF'}s_1\text{'Legacy'}y} * \text{v\_sep}_{r_1\text{'RegAF'}s_1\text{'Legacy'}y\text{'eyfirst'}f}$$

$$\forall (r_1, s_1, y, f) \in \text{s\_ireg} \ni cy > \text{cyfirst} \wedge (\text{fyfirst} < fy < \text{fyfirst} + 31) \wedge (cy \geq fy - \text{fyfirst})$$

12. Non-legacy affiliations to AFR are less than specified fraction of separations (all non-legacy affiliations go into ARC ADSC population)

$$\sum_{\substack{r_2 \in \text{s\_rcat} \\ s_2 \in \text{s\_icat} \\ p \in \text{s\_pop} \\ e \in \text{s\_ey} \\ \ni (r_1, \text{RegAF}, s_1, p, r_2, \text{AFR}, s_2, \text{ADSC}) \in \text{s\_allow\_afil} \\ \wedge p \neq \text{'Legacy'}}} \text{v\_afil}_{r_1\text{'RegAF'}s_1 p r_2\text{'AFR'}s_2\text{'ADSC'}yef}$$

$$\leq \text{p\_angrate}_{r_1\text{'RegAF'}s_1\text{'ADSC'}y}$$

$$* \sum_{\substack{p \in \text{s\_pop} \\ e \in \text{s\_ey} \\ \ni (r_1, \text{RegAF}, s_1, pyef) \in \text{s\_inv} \\ \wedge y \geq e \wedge p \neq \text{'Legacy'}}} \text{v\_sep}_{r_1\text{'RegAF'}s_1 pyef}$$

$$\forall (r_1, s_1, y, f) \in \text{s\_ireg} \ni cy > \text{cyfirst} \wedge (\text{fyfirst} < fy < \text{fyfirst} + 31) \wedge (cy \geq fy - \text{fyfirst})$$

13. Affiliations in each inventory category do not exceed separations

$$\sum_{\substack{r_2 \in \text{s\_rcat} \\ c_2 \in \text{s\_compo} \\ s_2 \in \text{s\_icat} \\ p_2 \in \text{s\_pop} \\ \ni (r_1, \text{'RegAF'}, s_1, p_1, r_2, c_2, s_2, p_2) \in \text{s\_allow\_afil} \\ \wedge c \geq e}} \text{v\_afil}_{r_1\text{'RegAF'}s_1 p_1 r_2 c_2 s_2 p_2, y, e, f} \leq \text{v\_sep}_{r_1\text{'RegAF'}s_1 p_1, y, e, f}$$

$$\forall (r_1, s_1, p_1, y, e, f) \in \text{s\_ireg\_ey} \ni y > \text{cyfirst} \wedge y \geq e \wedge f > \text{fyfirst}$$
$$\wedge \neg (p = \text{Legacy} \wedge (f \geq \text{fyfirst} + 31 \vee e > \text{eyfirst} \vee y < f - \text{fyfirst}))$$
$$\wedge \neg (p = \text{Legacy} \wedge (y \geq \text{eylast} + f - \text{fyfirst}))$$

14. Sum affiliations and palace chase over all destinations and cyos

$$\sum_{\substack{r_2 \in \text{s\_rcat} \\ c_2 \in \text{s\_compo} \\ s_2 \in \text{s\_icat} \\ p_1 \in \text{s\_pop} \\ p_2 \in \text{s\_pop} \\ y \in \text{s\_cy} \\ e \in \text{s\_ey} \\ \ni (r_1,c_1,s_1,p_1,r_2,c_2,s_2,p_2) \in \text{s\_allow\_afil} \\ \wedge y \geq e}} \text{v\_afil}_{r_1 c_1 s_1 p_1 r_2 c_2 s_2 p_2, y, e, f}$$

$$+ \sum_{\substack{r_2 \in \text{s\_rcat} \\ c_2 \in \text{s\_compo} \\ s_2 \in \text{s\_icat} \\ p_1 \in \text{s\_pop} \\ p_2 \in \text{s\_pop} \\ y \in \text{s\_cy} \\ e \in \text{s\_ey} \\ \ni (r_1,c_1,s_1,p_1,r_2,c_2,s_2,p_2) \in \text{s\_allow\_afil} \\ \wedge y \geq e}} \text{v\_palace}_{r_1 c_1 s_1 p_1 r_2 c_2 s_2 p_2, y, e, f}$$

$$= \text{v\_aforig}_{r_1 c_1 s_1 f}$$

$$\forall (r_1, c_1, s_1, f) \in \text{s\_afil\_orig\_fy} \ni fy > \text{fyfirst}$$

15. Penalize deviation of affiliations and palace chase from historical distribution of affiliation paths

$$\text{p\_allow\_afil}_{r_1 c_1 s_1 \text{'Legacy'} r_2 c_2 s_2 \text{'Legacy'}} * \text{v\_aforig}_{r_1 c_1 s_1 f}$$

$$- \sum_{\substack{p_1 \in \text{s\_pop} \\ p_2 \in \text{s\_pop} \\ y \in \text{s\_cy} \\ e \in \text{s\_ey} \\ \ni (r_1,p_1,p_2) \in \text{s\_afil\_flow} \\ \wedge y \geq e}} \text{v\_afil}_{r_1 c_1 s_1 p_1 r_2 c_2 s_2 p_2, y, e, f}$$

$$- \sum_{\substack{p_1 \in \text{s\_pop} \\ p_2 \in \text{s\_pop} \\ y \in \text{s\_cy} \\ e \in \text{s\_ey} \\ \ni (r_1,p_1,p_2) \in \text{s\_afil\_flow} \\ \wedge y \geq e}} \text{v\_palace}_{r_1 c_1 s_1 p_1 r_2 c_2 s_2 p_2, y, e, f}$$

$$= \text{v\_afpos}_{r_1 c_1 s_1 r_2 c_2 s_2 f} - \text{v\_afneg}_{r_1 c_1 s_1 r_2 c_2 s_2 f}$$

$$\forall (r_1, c_1, s_1, r_2, c_2, s_2, f) \in \text{s\_balafil} \ni f > \text{fyfirst}$$

16. Distribute programmed transitions over populations and entry years

$$\sum_{\substack{p_1 \in \text{s\_pop} \\ p_2 \in \text{s\_pop} \\ e \in \text{s\_ey} \\ \ni (r_1,c_1,s_1,p_1,r_2,c_2,s2,p_2,y,e,f) \in \text{s\_forcetransspop}}} \text{v\_force\_trans}_{r_1 c_1 s_1 p_1 r_2 c_2 s_2 p_2, y, e, f}$$

$$= \text{p\_force\_trans}_{r_1 c_1 s_1 p_1 r_2 c_2 s_2 p_2, y, f}$$

$$\forall(r_1, c_1, s_1, r_2, c_2, s_2, y, f) \in \text{s\_force\_trans}$$

17. Population shift affects current year inventory, so it can only be defined in terms of previous year's inventory. This constraint is very similar to the inventory balance constraint that follows, because it essentially solves for the number of pilots who would have continued past the shift point so that the inventory balance constraint can move them across populations.

$$
\begin{aligned}
\text{v\_popshift}_{r_1 c_1 s_1 p_1 y e f} = {} & \text{p\_shift}_{p_1 y e} * \text{v\_inv}_{r_1 c_1 s_1 p_1 y - 1 e f - 1} \\
& - \text{v\_sep}_{r_1 c_1 s_1 p_1 y e f} \\
& + \text{p\_dstent}_{r_1 c_1 s_1 p_1 y e} * \text{v\_ent}_{r_1 c_1 s_1 p_1 f} \\
& + \sum_{\substack{(r_2 c_2 s_2 p_2) \in \text{s\_ivld} \\ \ni (r_2, c_2, s2, p_2, r_1, c_1, s_1, p_1) \in \text{s\_allow\_afil}}} \text{v\_afil}_{r_2 c_2 s_2 p_2 r_1 c_1 s_1 p_1 y e f} \\
& + \sum_{\substack{(r_2 c_2 s_2 p_2) \in \text{s\_ivld} \\ \ni (r_2, c_2, s2, p_2, r_1, c_1, s_1, p_1, y, e, f) \in \text{s\_force\_trans\_pop}}} \text{v\_force\_trans}_{r_2 c_2 s_2 p_2 r_1 c_1 s_1 p_1 y e f} \\
& - \sum_{\substack{(r_2 c_2 s_2 p_2) \in \text{s\_ivld} \\ \ni (r_1, c_1, s_1, p_1, r_2, c_2, s2, p_2, y, e, f) \in \text{s\_force\_trans\_pop}}} \text{v\_force\_trans}_{r_1 c_1 s_1 p_1 r_2 c_2 s_2 p_2 y e f} \\
& + \sum_{\substack{(r_2 c_2 s_2 p_2) \in \text{s\_ivld} \\ \ni (r_2, c_2, s2, p_2, r_1, c_1, s_1, p_1, y, e, f) \in \text{s\_trans\_afil}}} \text{v\_palace}_{r_2 c_2 s_2 p_2 r_1 c_1 s_1 p_1 y e f} \\
& - \sum_{\substack{(r_2 c_2 s_2 p_2) \in \text{s\_ivld} \\ \ni (r_1, c_1, s_1, p_1, r_2, c_2, s2, p_2, y, e, f) \in \text{s\_trans\_afil}}} \text{v\_palace}_{r_1 c_1 s_1 p_1 r_2 c_2 s_2 p_2 y e f}
\end{aligned}
$$

$$\forall(r_1, c_1, s_1, p_1, y, e, f) \in \text{s\_inv} \ni y > \text{cyfirst} \land y \geq \land f > \text{fyfirst} + \text{windopen})$$
$$\land((p_1 = \text{Prewin} \land y = (e + \text{windopen})) \lor (p_1 = \text{Window} \land y = e + \text{adsclength}))$$

51

18. Inventory balance: $\text{Inv}(t+1) = \text{Inv}(t) + \text{Gains} - \text{Losses}$

$$\text{v\_inv}_{r_1 c_1 s_1 p_1 y e f} = \text{v\_inv}_{r_1 c_1 s_1 p_1 y - 1 e f - 1}$$

$$- \text{v\_sep}_{r_1 c_1 s_1 p_1 y e f}$$

$$- \text{v\_popshift}_{r_1 c_1 s_1 p_1 y e f}$$

$$+ \text{p\_dstent}_{r_1 c_1 s_1 p_1 y e} * \text{v\_ent}_{r_1 c_1 s_1 p_1 f}$$

$$+ \sum_{\substack{p_0 \in \text{s\_pop} \\ \forall (r_1, c_1, p_0, p_1) \in \text{s\_pflow}}} \text{v\_popshift}_{r_1 c_1 s_1 p_0 y e f}$$

$$+ \sum_{\substack{(r_2 c_2 s_2 p_2) \in \text{s\_ivld} \\ \ni (r_2, c_2, {}_s 2, p_2, r_1, c_1, s_1, p_1) \in \text{s\_allow\_afil}}} \text{v\_afil}_{r_2 c_2 s_2 p_2 r_1 c_1 s_1 p_1 y e f}$$

$$+ \sum_{\substack{(r_2 c_2 s_2 p_2) \in \text{s\_ivld} \\ \ni (r_2, c_2, {}_s 2, p_2, r_1, c_1, s_1, p_1, y, e, f) \in \text{s\_force\_trans\_pop}}} \text{v\_force\_trans}_{r_2 c_2 s_2 p_2 r_1 c_1 s_1 p_1 y e f}$$

$$- \sum_{\substack{(r_2 c_2 s_2 p_2) \in \text{s\_ivld} \\ \ni (r_1, c_1, s_1, p_1, r_2, c_2, {}_s 2, p_2, y, e, f) \in \text{s\_force\_trans\_pop}}} \text{v\_force\_trans}_{r_1 c_1 s_1 p_1 r_2 c_2 s_2 p_2 y e f}$$

$$+ \sum_{\substack{(r_2 c_2 s_2 p_2) \in \text{s\_ivld} \\ \ni (r_2, c_2, {}_s 2, p_2, r_1, c_1, s_1, p_1, y, e, f) \in \text{s\_trans\_afil}}} \text{v\_palace}_{r_2 c_2 s_2 p_2 r_1 c_1 s_1 p_1 y e f}$$

$$- \sum_{\substack{(r_2 c_2 s_2 p_2) \in \text{s\_ivld} \\ \ni (r_1, c_1, s_1, p_1, r_2, c_2, {}_s 2, p_2, y, e, f) \in \text{s\_trans\_afil}}} \text{v\_palace}_{r_1 c_1 s_1 p_1 r_2 c_2 s_2 p_2 y e f}$$

$$\forall (r_1, c_1, s_1, p_1, y, e, f) \in \text{s\_inv} \ni y > \text{cyfirst} \wedge y \geq e \wedge f > \text{fyfirst}$$
$$\wedge \neg (p = \text{Legacy} \wedge (f \geq \text{fyfirst} + 30 \vee e > \text{eyfirst} \vee cy < f - \text{fyfirst})$$
$$\wedge \neg (p \neq \text{Legacy} \wedge (y \geq \text{eylast} + f - \text{fyfirst}))$$

19. All RegAF communities must palace chase a minimum of 2 percent of eligible pilots each year.

$$\sum_{\substack{r_2 \in \text{s\_rcat} \\ c_2 \in \text{s\_compo} \\ s_2 \in \text{s\_icat} \\ p_2 \in \text{s\_pop} \\ y \in \text{s\_cy} \\ e \in \text{s\_ey} \\ \forall (('Plt'),('RegAF'),s_1,('Window'),r_2,c_2,s_2,p_2) \\ \in \text{s\_allow\_afil}}} \text{v\_palace},_{\text{Plt''RegAF'}s_1\text{'Window'}r_2 c_2 s_2 p_2 y e f} \geq$$

$$\frac{0.02}{1 - 0.02} * \sum_{\substack{y \in \text{s\_cy} \\ e \in \text{s\_ey}}} \text{v\_inv'}_{\text{Plt''RegAF'}s_1\text{'Window'}y e f}$$

$$\forall (s_1, f) \in \text{s\_palace\_min} \ni y \geq e$$

Boundary conditions

1. Initial inventories equal user-specified parameters:

$$\text{v\_inv}_{rcsp\text{'cyfirst'}ef} = 0 \qquad \forall (r,c,s,p,e,f) \in \text{s\_aginv\_ey} \wedge f > \text{fyfirst}$$

$$\text{v\_inv}_{rcspye\text{'fyfirst'}} = \text{p\_initinv}_{rcspye} \qquad \forall (r,c,s,p,y,e) \in \text{s\_init}$$

2. Separations at CYOS=0 are zero:

$$\text{v\_sep}_{rcsp\text{'cyfirst'}ef} = 0 \qquad \forall (r,c,s,p,e,f) \in \text{s\_aginv\_ey} \wedge f > \text{fyfirst}$$

3. Affiliations at CYOS=0 are zero:

$$\text{v\_afil}_{r_1 c_1 s_1 p_1 r_2 c_2 s_2 p_2 \text{'cyfirst'}ef} = 0 \quad \forall (r_1,c_1,s_1,p_1,r_2,c_2,s_2,p_2,y,e,f) \in \text{s\_trans\_afil} \wedge f > \text{fyfirst}$$

4. All Pilot production goes into PreWin population for RegAF, ADSC for ARC & RPA:

$$\text{v\_ent}_{rcspf} = 0 \qquad \forall (rcspf) \in \text{s\_ent} \wedge f > \text{fyfirst} \wedge c = \text{RegAF} \wedge r = \text{Plt} \wedge p \neq \text{PreWin}$$

$$\text{v\_ent}_{rcspf} = 0 \qquad \forall (rcspf) \in \text{s\_ent} \wedge f > \text{fyfirst} \wedge (c \neq \text{RegAF} \vee r = \text{RPA}) \wedge p \neq \text{PreWin}$$

5. Palace Chase transfers only allowed for RegAF Window Population:

$$\text{v\_palace}_{r_1 c_1 s_1 p_1 r_2 c_2 s_2 p_2 yef} = 0$$

$$\forall (r_1,c_1,s_1,p_1,r_2,c_2,s_2,p_2,y,e,f) \in \text{s\_trans\_afil}$$
$$\wedge \neg (p_1 = \text{Window} \wedge (f > \text{fyfirst} + \text{windopen}) \wedge (e + \text{windopen} \leq y < e + \text{adsclength}))$$

6. Fix as many values as possible to reduce computation time:

$$\text{v\_inv}_{rcspyef} = 0$$

$$\forall (rcspyef) \in \text{s\_inv} \wedge p = \text{Legacy} \wedge (f \geq \text{fyfirst} + 30 \vee e > \text{eyfirst} \vee y < f - \text{fyfirst})$$

$$\text{v\_inv}_{rcspyef} = 0 \qquad \forall (rcspyef) \in \text{s\_inv} \wedge p \neq \text{Legacy} \wedge (y \geq \text{eylast} + f - \text{fyfirst})$$

$$\text{v\_sep}_{rcspyef} = 0$$

$$\forall (rcspyef) \in \text{s\_inv} \land p = \text{Legacy} \land (f \geq \text{fyfirst} + 31 \lor e > \text{eyfirst} \lor y < f - \text{fyfirst})$$

$$\text{v\_sep}_{rcspyef} = 0 \qquad \forall (rcspyef) \in \text{s\_inv} \land p \neq \text{Legacy} \land (y \geq \text{eylast} + f - \text{fyfirst})$$

$$\text{v\_afil}_{r_1 c_1 s_1 p_1 r_2 c_2 s_2 p_2 yef} = 0$$

$$\forall (r_1, c_1, s_1, p_1, r_2, c_2, s_2, p_2, y, e, f) \in \text{s\_trans\_afil}$$
$$\land p_1 = \text{Legacy} \land (f \geq \text{fyfirst} + 31 \lor e > \text{eyfirst} \lor y < f - \text{fyfirst})$$

$$\text{v\_afil}_{r_1 c_1 s_1 p_1 r_2 c_2 s_2 p_2 yef} = 0$$

$$\forall (r_1, c_1, s_1, p_1, r_2, c_2, s_2, p_2, y, e, f) \in \text{s\_trans\_afil} \land p_1 \neq \text{Legacy} \land (y \geq \text{eylasrt} + f\text{fyfirst})$$

$$\text{v\_inv}_{rcspyef} = 0$$

$$\forall (rcspyef) \in \text{s\_inv}$$
$$\land (\neg (p \neq \text{'Prewin'} \land cy = (e + \text{windopen})) \land \neg (p \neq \text{windopen} \land y = (e + \text{adsclength})))$$
$$\lor fy < \text{fyfirst} + \text{windopen}$$

7. We limited the range of values where constraints apply to reduce the computational burden, so decision variables must be constrained to zero where constraints do not apply:

$$\text{v\_inv}_{rcspyef} = 0 \qquad \forall (rcspyef) \in \text{s\_inv} \land y < e \land f > \text{fyfirst}$$

$$\text{v\_sep}_{rcspyef} = 0 \qquad \forall (rcspyef) \in \text{s\_inv} \land y < e$$

$$\text{v\_afil}_{r_1 c_1 s_1 p_1 r_2 c_2 s_2 p_2 \text{'cyfirst'}ef} = 0 \qquad \forall (r_1, c_1, s_1, p_1, r_2, c_2, s_2, p_2, y, e, f) \in \text{s\_trans\_afil} \land y < e$$

$$\text{v\_afil}_{r_1 c_1 s_1 p_1 r_2 c_2 s_2 p_2 \text{'cyfirst'}ef} = 0$$

$$\forall (r_1, c_1, s_1, p_1, r_2, c_2, s_2, p_2, y, e, f) \in \text{s\_force\_trans\_pop}$$
$$\land (p_1 = \text{Leacy} \land (f \geq \text{fyfirst} + 30 \lor e > \text{eyfirst} \lor cy < f - \text{fyfirst}))$$
$$\lor (p_1 \neq \text{Legacy} \land (y \geq \text{eylast} + f - \text{fyfirst}))$$
$$\lor y < e$$

References

Air Force Instruction 36-2107, *Personnel: Active Duty Service Commitments (ADSC)*, Washington, D.C.: Department of the Air Force, April 30, 2012. As of February 22, 2018: http://static.e-publishing.af.mil/production/1/af_a1/publication/afi36-2107/afi36-2107.pdf

Air Force Instruction 36-3205, *Personnel: Applying for the Palace Chase and Palace Front Programs*, Washington, D.C.: Department of the Air Force, October 10, 2003, Incorporating Change 2, November 12, 2009. As of February 22, 2018: http://static.e-publishing.af.mil/production/1/af_a1/publication/afi36-3205/afi36-3205.pdf

Gates, Susan M., Beth Roth, Sinduja Srinivasan, and Lindsay Daugherty, *Analyses of the Department of Defense Acquisition Workforce: Update to Methods and Results Through FY 2011*, Santa Monica, Calif.: RAND Corporation, RR-110-OSD, 2013. As of February 22, 2018: https://www.rand.org/pubs/research_reports/RR110.html

Grosso, Lieutenant General Gina M., testimony before the U.S. House of Representatives Armed Services Committee, March 29, 2017, in *Military Pilot Shortage: Hearings before the Subcommittee on Military Personnel, Committee on Armed Services, U.S. House of Representatives, 115th Congress, First Session*, Washington, D.C.: U.S. Government Publishing Office, 2017.

Harrington, Lisa M., James H. Bigelow, Alexander D. Rothenberg, James Pita, and Paul Emslie, *A Methodology for Modeling the Flow of Military Personnel Across Air Force Active and Reserve Components*, Santa Monica, Calif.: RAND Corporation, RR-825-AF, 2016. As of February 22, 2018: https://www.rand.org/pubs/research_reports/RR825.html

Hastie, Trevor, Robert Tibshirani, and Jerome Friedman, *The Elements of Statistical Learning: Data Mining, Inference, and Prediction*, 2nd ed., Springer Science and Business Media, LLC, 2009.

Mattock, Michael G., James Hosek, Beth J. Asch, and Rita Karam, *Retaining U.S. Air Force Pilots When the Civilian Demand for Pilots Is Growing*, Santa Monica, Calif.: RAND Corporation, RR-1455-AF, 2016. As of February 22, 2018: https://www.rand.org/pubs/research_reports/RR1455.html

McGee, Michael, *Air Transport Pilot Supply and Demand: Current State and Effects of Recent Legislation*, Santa Monica, Calif.: RAND Corporation, RGSD-351, 2015. As of February 22,

2018:
https://www.rand.org/pubs/rgs_dissertations/RGSD351.html

Ridgeway, Greg, "Generalized Boosted Models: A Guide to the GBM Package," *The Comprehensive R Archive Network*, 2007. As of July 7, 2017:
https://rweb.stat.umn.edu/R/site-library/gbm/doc/gbm.pdf

Ridgeway, Greg, David Madigan, and Thomas Richardson, "Boosting Methodology for Regression Problems," in D. Heckerman and J. Whittaker, eds., *Proceedings of Artificial Intelligence and Statistics '99*, 1999, pp. 152–161.

Robbert, Albert A., Anthony D. Rosello, C. R. Anderegg, John A. Ausink, James H. Bigelow, Bill Taylor, and James Pita, *Reducing Air Force Fighter Pilot Shortages*, Santa Monica, Calif.: RAND Corporation, RR-1113-AF, 2015. As of February 22, 2018:
https://www.rand.org/pubs/research_reports/RR1113.html

Skowronski, Will, "Pilot Shortage, Back with a Vengeance," *Air Force Magazine*, August 2016. As of August 8, 2017:
http://www.airforcemag.com/MagazineArchive/Pages/2016/August%202016/Pilot-Shortage-Back-With-a-Vengeance.aspx

Sweeney, Nolan, *Predicting Active Duty Air Force Pilot Attrition Given an Anticipated Increase in Major Airline Pilot Hiring*, Santa Monica, Calif.: RAND Corporation, RGSD-338, 2015. As of February 22, 2018:
https://www.rand.org/pubs/rgs_dissertations/RGSD338.html

Taylor, Bill, Craig Moore, and Charles Robert Roll, Jr., *The Air Force Pilot Shortage: A Crisis for Operational Units?* Santa Monica, Calif.: RAND Corporation, MR-1204-AF, 2000. As of February 22, 2018:
https://www.rand.org/pubs/monograph_reports/MR1204.html

Terry, Tara L., James H. Bigelow, James Pita, Jerry Sollinger, and Paul Emslie, *User's Guide for the Total Force Blue-Line (TFBL) Model*, Santa Monica, Calif.: RAND Corporation, TL-233-AF, 2017. As of February 22, 2018:
https://www.rand.org/pubs/tools/TL233.html

Terry, Tara L., Jeremy M. Eckhause, Michael McGee, James H. Bigelow, Paul Emslie, and Jerry M. Sollinger, *Projecting Air Force Rated Officer Inventory Across the Total Force: Total Force Blue Line Model for Rated Officer Management*, Santa Monica, Calif.: RAND Corporation, forthcoming.